EQUALITY OF OPPORTUNITY IN IRISH THIRD-LEVEL INSTITUTIONS

Proceedings of a Forum held September, 1990

in University College Cork

(Organised by the Committee on Equality of
Opportunity University College, Cork.)

Edited by Caroline Fennell and Maire Mulcahy

Left to Right:

Dr. Frances Ruane, Trinity College, Dublin; **Dr. Michael Mortell,** President, University College Cork; **Prof. Maire Mulcahy,** Vice-President, University College Cork and Chairperson, Committee on Equality of Opportunity; **Michael F. Kelleher,** Finance Officer and Secretary, University College Cork; **Mary Clark-Glass,** Equal Opportunities Commission, Northern Ireland; **Dr. Patrick Clancy,** University College Dublin; **Prof. Helen Burke,** University College Dublin; **John Hayden,** Secretary, Higher Education Authority; **Dr. Caroline Fennell,** University College Cork; **Dearbhal Ni Charthaigh,** Thomond College.

INTRODUCTION

This publication contains the text of papers presented at the **Forum on Equality of Opportunity in Third Level Institutions** which was hosted by the Committee on Equality of Opportunity, University College Cork, in September 1990.

The Forum was organised in order to examine the position in relation to equality of opportunity among students and staff in Ireland, North and South. It was hoped to identify prime issues, share experiences and examine various responses and initiatives taken in institutions, and society generally, to promote equality of opportunity.

During the final discussion session of the Forum, it was mooted that the Forum be sustained as an ongoing organisation. A follow-up meeting of a group, representative of all the participating interests and institutions, was held in University College Cork, in November 1990. It was agreed the Forum should constitute an umbrella network facilitating for the sharing of information and ideas in relation to (a) equality-related issues; and (b) women's studies. General principles and aspirations to inform that development were felt to include the following:

:   the network should focus on third level;

:   "equality" should include gender-related and socio-economic, as well as other issues;

:   the network should link into existing and future international networks;

:   the network should be inclusive of all women students, as well as all categories of women staff: academic and non-academic, part-time and full-time in Ireland, North and South;

: the network framework should enable component individuals and groups to speak as one group;

: the network should build up a data-base for information

: the network should be known as the Women's Forum on Equality of Opportunity in Third Level Institutions.

On a practical level it was felt that until funding is obtained in support of the Forum, the Forum should concentrate on holding the Annual Forum meeting, to be organised by a volunteer Convenor, where role and venue rotates from year to year among the membership.

Efforts would immediately be made to attract funding for the Forum to fund an Organiser, data base, and office.

A priority objective would be the declaration and implementation of a Policy of Equality of Opportunity by each Irish third level institution.

Caroline Fennell and Maire Mulcahy

The organisers of the first Forum gratefully acknowledge financial support from the EC Equality Unit for the Forum meeting, and from the Higher Education Authority for the publication of the proceedings.

CONTENTS

SPEAKERS

1. **Helen Burke** is Associate Professor of Social Administration and Social Work in University College Dublin (UCD). She was first elected to the Governing Body by the graduates of UCD in 1985, and is Convenor of the Governing Body's Equal Opportunities Committee. She also chairs the Board of Studies for the Postgraduate Programme in Women's Studies in the Women's Education Research and Resource Centre in UCD.

2. **Patrick Clancy** is a Statutory Lecturer in the Department of Sociology, University College Dublin. His main research has been in the area of higher education. During the past ten years he has completed two national studies of the pattern of participation in higher education. These studies have been funded and published by the Higher Education Authority. Other research interests include sociology of education, Irish social structure and the sociology of the family. He is currently joint editor of the Economic and Social Review.

3. **Mary Clark-Glass** has been Chairperson and Chief Executive of the Equal Opprotunities Commission for Northern Ireland since 1984. A Law graduate, she previously held the post of Lecturer in Law at the College of Business Studies in Belfast. She specialised in mercantile law and the law relating to consumers. From 1978-1981, she was a member of the National Consumer Council, and from 1978-1982 she was a U.K. representative on the EEC's Economic and Social Committee. On retiring from the National Consumer Council in 1981, Mary Clark-Glass was appointed Chairperson of the Lisburn Social Security and Northern Ireland Local Appeal Tribunal, but resigned

on her appointment to the Equal Opportunities Commission.

4. **Catherine Fitzpatrick** is an Arts graduate of University College Cork. She teaches French and English in the Patrician Academy, Mallow, Co. Cork. Since 1988 she has been a member of the ASTI Equality Committee.

5. **John Hayden** B.Sc. (Econ.) has been Secretary (Chief Executive) of the Higher Education Authority since 1983. For the previous ten years he was employed by the Authority in a variety of posts on research into educational issues, the establishment of a data base on higher education and recurrent expenditure procedures. Previous to 1973 he was employed by RTE on work study/operations research, by Bord Failte on market surveys and by McMullen's Kosangas in Industrial Sales. Mr. Hayden is a B.Sc. (Econ.) graduate of London University in Economics and Statistics.

6. **Sylvia Meehan** has been Chief Executive of the Equality Employment Agency since 1977. She is former Vice-Principal of Cabinteely Community School. She has been a leading campaigner for equality of opportunity in employment and is a former President of the EC Advisory Committee on Equal Opportunities between Men and Women.

7. **Dearbhal Ni Charthaigh** is a Lecturer in the Education Department, Thomond College, and Co-Director of the Centre for Studies in Gender and Education, and Joint Coordinator for the Graduate Diploma in Women's Studies in the University Limerick. She is Consultant to the European Commission on Equal Opportunities in Education and Training, and to the Department of Education on equality, as well as Presidency expert to the Education Committee of the E.C. She is also responsible for European co-ordination of the TENET

programme. She is Coordinator of the Women in Higher Education Network (WHEN), and author of many articles and papers in education and women's studies.

8. **Frances Ruane** an Economics graduate of UCD and Oxford, is a Lecturer in Economics and Fellow of Trinity College Dublin. She is a Council Member of Economic and Social Studies, Research Director of the, Foundation for Fiscal Studies, and Economics Editor of the Economic and Social Review. She served as a Committee member on the Higher Education Authority's Committee on the Status of Women in Third-Level Education. She chaired the Committee on the Position of Academic Women in TCD in 1988-1989, and since 1990 has been a member of the TCD Committee on Equality of Opportunity for Academics.

9. **Stuart Spence** is a Law graduate of Queen's University, Belfast and is currently studying part-time for a Masters Degree in Discrimination Law. He spent several years with the Fair Employment Agency as a Conciliation Officer, and left in 1989 to set up the Equal Opportunities Unit with the Southern Health and Social Services Board. In April 1990, he was appointed as Equal Opportunities Executive at QUB.

EQUALITY OF OPPORTUNITY IN IRISH THIRD-LEVEL INSTITUTIONS

John Hayden

[This paper outlines the position on equality among students and staff in third level education, and the ways in which the Higher Education Authority promotes and monitors equality of opportunity, a responsibility assigned to it under the H.E.A. Act.

Ed.]

1. The Authority has always maintained an interest in promoting equality of opportunity in third-level education in Ireland. Indeed, the Higher Education Authority Act assigns to the Authority the general function of promoting the attainment of equality of opportunity in higher education.

2. To this end, the Authority has commissioned a number of major studies which have highlighted trends in participation in higher education, identifying inequalities where they occur at regional, socio-economic, or gender levels. These studies include:

    Higher Education in Dublin: a study of some emerging needs by Patrick Clancy and Ciaran Benson (1978); and

    Participation in Higher Education: A National Survey (1982) and Who Goes to College? (1988) by Patrick Clancy.

3. The findings of these studies have been widely disseminated and have formed the basis for decisions such as the establishment of the Tallaght RTC. In addition, the Authority's annual publication of student statistics helps to identify inequalities where they occur and to monitor progress. Statistics are compiled in relation to undergraduates, postgraduates, areas of study, geographical origin, socio-economic origins.

4. The attainment of equality of opportunity for school-leavers in third-level education is not something which can be easily achieved by third-level institutions in isolation. It almost certainly will require changes at second-level and even earlier. However initiatives taken by the Colleges in recent years, such as the holding of 'open days' for second-level pupils, are to be applauded and it is hoped that they will continue. The vital importance of student support systems must be taken into account. For this reason, it is gratifying to note the Minister for Education's recent announcement of the reduction of the basic academic requirement for a higher education grant to two honours.

5. Other worthwhile steps taken in this area by individual colleges include the establishment by the University of Limerick of an 'Introduction to University' programme which provides an early opportunity for senior cycle students, male and female, to explore career options. The University has also established a matriculation examination in Mathematics which facilitates entry from school applicants who may not have had the chance to do Honours Maths at school.

6. In addition to maintaining an interest in the attainment of equality of opportunity among third-level students, the Authority has also been active in the area of staff recruitment and promotion among the colleges. The latter has for many years been a very

2

controversial area. At the request of the Minister for Education in 1985, a working party was established to determine the position of women academics in third-level education in Ireland after the publication of Ailbhe Smyth's imaginative study.

7. This group reported early in 1987. Its report, <u>Women Academics in Ireland</u>, is based on two major surveys: firstly, the analysis of statistical data received from the universities and other institutions designated to the Authority; secondly, a postal survey of all female academics (and a matched sample of males) which provided detailed information on career patterns, backgrounds, and attitudes to a number of key career determinants. Professor Brendan Whelan of the Economic and Social Research Institute conducted the latter survey.

8. The findings of these surveys have been widely disseminated and are too lengthy to report in full here. Briefly, it was established that women comprised 14.5% of full-time faculty in the universities and 18% in the other designated institutions. This was in sharp contrast to their representation in the student body, where at the time they accounted for 46% of full-time students. The percentages masked substantial variations between different lecturing grades: for instance, in the universities women comprised only 2% of full Professors and 5% of Associate Professors. They were more highly represented in the junior grades and concentrated in fields of study where expansion was less rapid. (It should be noted that the Committee found no evidence of overtly discriminatory rules and procedures).

9. The Authority undertook to monitor progress in the universities and other institutions which it funds, and

in 1989 available data on overall numbers of academic staff were examined.

10. Little change, unfortunately, was evident in the figures. As was acknowledged by the Authority at the time, the difficult economic circumstances of the late 1980s made for restrictions on staff recruitment, and obviously this had retarded any progress. Some positive signs, however, included the increased percentages of women academic staff in the faculties of Medicine, Veterinary Medicine and Agricultural and Dairy Science.

11. It would however be a counsel of despair not to acknowledge that even since 1988, the year the Authority's Report was published, there have been significant waves in the Colleges towards equality of opportunity, both in the recruitment of students in the area of gender equality, and on the appointment of and conditions of service of staff, matters which are related. Publications of guides to colleges and courses, including student information booklets are couched in such terms as to avoid gender discrimination. Particularly useful in the general area of promoting equality of opportunity are the open days organised by faculties and departments. There have been encouraging responses to a number of special measures for Leaving Certificate students, in relation to entry to courses which have apparent imbalance in the gender mix of students. Dublin City University organised a weekend school to introduce students to Physics and other sciences; the School of Electronic Engineering holds a week-long school to introduce students to Engineering and Technology. The University of Limerick in its Introduction to University Programme provides an opportunity for senior cycle students of both sexes to explore career options. This University also provides a special Mathematics

examination to facilitate entry from school applicants who may not have the chance to do Higher Mathematics at school - this obviously is of great potential assistance to female applicants. Trinity College Dublin has like the five older university institutions a majority of female entrants to its courses overall. That College has a policy of highlighting the achievements of women in Engineering, Mathematics and the Natural Sciences in its liaison with schools and in particular in the presentations made in the course of annual Open Days for schools in the faculties of Engineering and Systems Sciences and of Science. Given the changes which are occurring in relation to the ordination of women in several Christian churches, it is interesting to note that courses in Theology are open to men and women in Trinity College and that there are students of both sexes in the Theology course for ordinands of the Church of Ireland. While the courses have a different purpose, it is interesting to note that the majority of students on the Bachelor of Theology/Arts course in St. Patrick's College, Maynooth and in the Mater Dei Institute are women. It seems to me that with the exception of engineering, where there is a marked lack of women students, and the para medical disciplines, where the opposite situation prevails, that there has been an appreciable lessening of gender imbalance in the student body.

12. Official committees have been established in many of the university institutions to investigate the position in regard to the status of women academic and non-academic staff also. (The concentration on women academics only, both in the HEA study and in other studies has been, perhaps unfairly, criticised on a number of occasions). Matters identified vary from College to College but in general the College authorities strongly affirm their commitment to ensuring equality

of opportunity for all their employees. The Colleges are conscious of the need not alone to have employment policies, procedures and practices which do not discriminate on the grounds of sex but also of the need to promote full equality of opportunity between men and women. Several colleges have advised the Authority that such policies are in many cases kept under constant review to ensure that they actively promote gender equality. Certainly some aspire or claim to aspire to ideal measures in this regard. Another college has advised us that their actions in this regard include the following:

(i) It is proposed to establish a Committee to monitor and report annually on the position of women academics in College;

(ii) Sexist language will be removed from documentation;

(iii) Various steps are being taken to ensure that there will be a fair proportion of junior staff and female staff on Committees;

(iv) Various steps are to be taken to ensure that part-time staff are treated equitably;

(v) Various steps are being taken to re-circulate information on employment matters such as Job-Sharing Schemes, Leaves of Absence, Career Breaks and so on;

(vi) The administration of the Maternity Leave regulations is to be reviewed. Also, the administration of the Day Nursery is to be reviewed.

A wide ranging series of measures relating to recruitment and promotion are under active consideration. These matters form part of the above report but it was felt they need further examination. In broad terms the following is envisaged:

(a)   An equality statement on all application forms (already in operation);

(b)   Consideration of such a statement in public advertisements;

(c)   Consideration of structuring nomination for Appointment Committees to ensure representation of both sexes;

(d)   Consideration of seminars and/or lectures by applicants as part of the recruitment selection process.

Another College Advises:

(a)   Recruitment and Selection:
All recruitment posts in the University are open to male and female applicants. Recruitment methods encourage applications from suitable candidates of both sexes. Interview Boards are comprised of individuals of both sexes. Short lists of interviewees are reviewed to ensure equity.

(b)   Mobility:
In particular, recognising the under-representation of women amongst Senior Academics, the University actively encourages female academic employees to engage in research and to achieve postgraduate qualifications which will rectify this under-representation and

maintain them on an equal footing with men when promotions are being considered. This encouragement takes the form of the payment of fees and providing the employee with teaching hours which recognise that the individual is engaging in research for a higher qualification.

(c) Training and Development:
Training and Development are equally available to all employees and there is no discrimination on the grounds of sex in relation to the opportunities available to each employee. To ensure that there are no impediments such as lack of academic qualification or training which would disadvantage female non-academic staff in particular in the promotions situation, female staff are actively encouraged to pursue evening degrees at the University or other Third Level Colleges. The initiatives taken by the University in this area relate to the payment of fees and the provision of examination and study leave.

13. The research difficulties of staff with family responsibilities are recognised as an important factor in gender equality among staff. Colleges have stressed the following to us in this regard.

Recognising that staff with family responsibilities may encounter some difficulties reconciling their work and family responsibilities, as a means of promoting gender equity, all staff, and female staff in particular, are made aware of the following:

(a) The Creche facilities available in the vicinity of the University;

(b) The University's Maternity Leave scheme;

(c)　Job Sharing Scheme available which enables female employees in particular, to combine home and work responsibilities.

The terms and conditions of appointment for all staff are the same, irrespective of race, creed or sex. Since its introduction the University Pension Scheme has included female staff in its Spouse's and Children's Scheme. The University has implemented maternity leave and leave for adoptive mothers. The University operates a policy whereby female members of staff who become pregnant can be relieved of certain duties if they so request.

14.　I quote these examples to show how the institutions illustrate progress being made on giving effect to the recommendations made by the Authority's Committee in 1987. Not all of them have, as yet, been implemented in each institution but at least some of them have been implemented in all institutions. A further sign of this progress in higher education is the approval and introduction of courses in Women's Studies at the University of Limerick and University College Dublin.

POLICY AND EXPERIENCES IN NORTHERN IRELAND

Mary Clark-Glass

[This paper gives an account of the task facing the Equal Opportunities Commission for Northern Ireland with regard to ensuring the elimination of discrimination between men and women in employment, together with strategies adopted to date.

Ed.]

The Equal Opportunities Commission for Northern Ireland came into existence on 1st September 1976. Its duties over fourteen years later are still the same:

(a)   To work towards the elimination of discrimination;

(b)   to promote equality of opportunity between men and women generally;

(c)   to keep under review the working of the Order and the Equal Pay Act and, when the Commission is so required by the Department, or otherwise thinks it necessary, draw up and submit to the Department proposals for amending them.

(Article 54 of the Sex Discrimination (Northern Ireland) Order, 1976)

As its First Annual Report set out:

The Commission is also vested with powers in relation to research and education; it may conduct formal investigations and, in the event of discrimination being found, may issue non-discrimination notices, a register of which must be made available to the public at the Commission's Offices.

The Commission has the sole right to initiate action in relation to persistent discrimination, discriminatory advertisements, and instructions or pressure to discriminate. It may assist a person in the preparation of a claim either under the Order or under the Equal Pay Act (Northern Ireland) 1970, where the claim raises a question of principle, is complex, or for any other special reason.

Legal action under the Order lies, in the case of employment, to Industrial Tribunals, and in all other cases, to the County Courts.

The Commission's present priorities, therefore, are drawn up and implemented with that statutory remit in mind. The general policy statement agreed by the Commission in 1990 states:

The Goal   The goal of the Commission is the achievement of equality of opportunity between women and men.

The Strategies Strategic enforcement of the sex discrimination and equal pay legislation is reaffirmed as the Commission's policy. This will be done by making full use of the Commission's statutory powers, as appropriate.

At the same time the Commission will continue to promote voluntary compliance with both the letter and spirit of the equality laws. The Commission will also keep the effectiveness of the legislation under review.

Areas   The Commission will continue to give priority to issues affecting the attainment of equality of opportunity for women in employment.

The seven issues identified by the Commission, where resources and work will be concentrated over the next three years, are:

Equal Pay
Contractual Terms
Working Parents
Non-Traditional Working Areas
Vertical De-Segregation
Education - The National Curriculum
Sexual Harassment.

(a)   Equal Pay

This is where inequality between women and men is most starkly seen. The continuing differential between men's and women's pay is a clear example not only of the lack of opportunity for women to obtain access to jobs of equal status to men, but also of the undervaluing of the demands of the jobs which women undertake.

The table below shows women's earnings vis-a-vis men's:

Average gross hourly earnings, excluding overtime, of full-time employees on adult rates in April of each year.

	Pence per hour					
	1974*	1979*	1974	1987	1988	1989
MEN	94.6	207.0	367.9	443.6	473.0	518.2
WOMEN	65.9	147.5	274.9	331.7	351.0	407.2
Women's Earnings as a percentage of men's	69.7	71.2	74.7	74.8	74.2	78.6

* Men aged 21 and over, women aged 18 and over

After nearly six years of the operation of the equal value provision, it is clear that the legislation has had virtually no impact on the pay differential between women's average earnings and men's average earnings.

In attempting to make equal pay between men and women a reality, the Commission is involved in assisting complainants in a number of significant claims covering both public and private sector concerns. The claims have far-reaching implications for pay structures, collective bargaining, job evaluation, and parity. Also, the claims have highlighted the inadequacy of the legislation, which has precluded successful claimants from receiving equal pay so far.

Recognising this inadequacy, the Commission has now drawn up and published a major policy paper 'The

Equal Pay Legislation: Recommendations for Change'. Amongst its recommendations the Commission recommends substantive legislative and procedural changes. These include the consolidation of the Equal Pay Act (Northern Ireland) 1970 with the Sex Discrimination (Northern Ireland) Order 1976 as amended, and the simplification of the regulations which accompany the Equal Value Amendment. The legislation should also be amended to implement the obligations laid down in European Law and recent rulings of the House of Lords. There are also recommendations which, if implemented, would simplify and speed up the progression of claims. The paper also recommends interim administrative changes, which could improve the operation of the legislation, pending the necessary Parliamentary process.

In addition to litigation, the Commission is involved in a number of major initiatives where employers and trade unions are carrying out audits of existing pay structures, and implementing job evaluation schemes as a means of addressing equal pay for work of equal value. This area of the Commission's work is developing as it is increasingly attempting to encourage the traditional collective bargaining structures to take the issue of equal value on board.

Obviously, there are difficulties. The issue often does not fit easily with the collective bargaining process where different trade unions represent segregated work areas and guard differentials which perpetuate unequal pay. In legal terms, there are also difficulties in addressing, through individual litigation, what is, in fact, a collective issue.

(b)   Contractual Terms

The less favourable statutory and contractual terms and protection afforded to part-time, temporary, or sub-contracted workers adversely impacts on women, as women predominate in these categories of workers. Widespread sex segregation in employment, has contributed to this situation.

The Commission is currently examining the way in which part-time workers in Northern Ireland are excluded from certain statutory protection. For example, whereas a person working over sixteen hours per week is protected against unfair dismissal once employed for more than two years, a person working eight to sixteen hours per week must be employed for five years before gaining similar protection. Someone working under eight hours per week can never gain protection, no matter how many years that person works for an employer. As the vast majority of part-time workers are women, it is clear that the existing United Kingdom law treats women less favourably than men. Indeed, the European Court of Justice in the Rinner Kuhn case, earlier this year has pointed out the unlawfulness of this in relation to sick pay.

Following the European case, the Equal Opportunities Commission in Great Britain has already sought leave to apply for Judicial Review of the Government's legislation, and the Equal Opportunities Commission for Northern Ireland is also taking appropriate action.

These challenges are an important part of the Commission's strategy, as there is a need not only to prevent erosion of existing rights but also to challenge the adequacy of those rights in the light of domestic and European legislation.

The draft European Directives on part-time and temporary work underline the position set out in the Rinner Kuhn case.

(c)   Working Parents

Such arrangements as career breaks, contractual maternity provision, parental leave, job sharing, and childcare are within this priority area. The role of women in child-bearing and child-rearing results in a major barrier to their equal treatment in the field of employment.

In the area of maternity rights, therefore, the Commission is currently very active. At present the rights and benefits of women workers in the United Kingdom are amongst the least beneficial in Europe, and the Commission is challenging the legality of the current contractual provisions in the Northern Ireland courts, which will impact on statutory provisions.

At present complaints relating to treatment at work and maternity comprise a substantial and growing part of the work of the Commission's Legal Team. Employers are confused between statutory maternity rights and the rights of women not to be discriminated against on the grounds of pregnancy. The Commission's publication 'Maternity Rights for Women at Work' is used widely by both employers and workers, and the next Equality Seminar (part of a series run for equality officers, personnel managers, etc.) in October will be concentrating on this topic.

The Commission strongly advocates the widespread introduction of a comprehensive choice of flexible working arrangement which will facilitate working parents to combine their domestic and work commitments. Within this context adequate high quality childcare is essential and the Commission, with other organisations in Northern Ireland, has been lobbying and working for an improvement in the existing abysmal childcare provisions in the province. Without such care, equality of opportunity between women and men will not be realised, and the low economic status of women will be perpetuated.

(d)   Non-Traditional Working Areas

Women continue to be employed in sex segregated areas of employment - the traditional 'female occupations'. The most recent Labour Force Survey shows that over half of the female workforce are in just three areas:

i.	Professionals in Education, Welfare, and health.	18.4%
ii.	Clerical and related.	25.4%
iii.	Catering, Cleaning, Hairdressing, and other personal services.	23.0%

Most of the work done by women is characterised by low pay, poor prospects, and generally low status. It is significant, in this context, to note that women in Northern Ireland are still significantly under-represented in science and technology subjects: Just over a quarter of students taking A Level physics are female; only 9% of students studying engineering and technology subjects are women.

Faced with a highly segregated labour market, the Commission's work to improve the status and conditions of 'women's' jobs remains of vital importance. By enforcing the sex discrimination and equal pay legislation through individual cases, and by being the primary body in Northern Ireland providing objective and reliable information on the nature and extent of sex inequality in society, the Commission strives to be a force for change. It also has the important task of educating employers, trade unions, and employees about the rights and obligations accruing from the legislation and, by its publications, research reports, seminars, numerous speaking engagements, and work with the media, the Commission constantly strives to ensure that information reaches as wide an audience as possible. Through its education and promotion programme, the Commission also works to change attitudes about the respective roles of women and men in society.

(e) Vertical De-Segregation

Even in areas where women workers predominate numerically (as above), women are disproportionately concentrated at the lower levels. Over the last few years the Commission has supported a number of significant cases, such.as those relating to teacher promotion. It has worked with the Northern Ireland Civil Service on equality of opportunity in the Civil Service and with employers ranging from the Royal Ulster Constabulary, the four Health and Social Services Boards, Northern Ireland Housing Executive, and Northern Ireland Railways, to Northern Ireland banks, insurance companies, and small employers. The Commission has also taken a close interest in the Youth Training Programme in Northern Ireland, commissioning research on sex equality in the Youth Training Programme, and is participating in a working group convened by the newly-created Training and Employment Agency.

The Commission's guide 'Making Changes for Women at Work: How to Implement an Equal Opportunities Programme' is part of its work in encouraging employers to implement affirmative action programmes. This publication ranges far beyond the problem of vertical de-segregation, as it draws together the Commission's advice on all aspects of the employment relationship, and sets it out in a step-by-step approach to the development of an equal opportunities programme. From the first step of issuing a policy statement, to the monitoring of a programme once in place, and to setting targets and timetables for achieving change, the booklet gives detailed guidance on the implementation of an equal opportunities programme. As soon as the booklet was printed it was in considerable demand and the Commission expects that, through its publication, the number of employers seeking the Commission's advice on the development of affirmative action programmes will increase greatly.

(f)　Education - The National Curriculum

The Commission's present priority area in relation to education is the National Curriculum, currently being introduced in stages into Northern Ireland. In the past the Commission has assisted and commissioned research into a number of areas including:

Northern Ireland Women in Higher Education (1981)
Science and Arts Subject Choices: A Sample Survey of Lower 6th Form Students in Northern Ireland (1985)
Attitudes to Women in Northern Ireland (1986)
Gender Differentiation in Infant Classes (1987)
Women in the Professions (1987).

Current research includes an examination of how the new General Certificate of Secondary Education mathematics examination provides equality of opportunity, plus a general study of the National Curriculum and possible gender implications. This study will examine the extent to which the meaningful provision of equality of opportunity for both sexes has been taken into account in the proposals and arrangements under the Education Reform (Northern Ireland) Order 1989, with particular reference to the curricula of the six areas of study, the six strands of learning (cross-curriculum themes), the procedures and methods of assessment and testing, and the guidance provided for schools on teaching and learning approaches.

19

The changes being introduced under the National Curriculum will affect the future prospects of all young people in the school system in Northern Ireland and the Commission is concerned to ensure that equality of opportunity between the sexes is provided comprehensively throughout the system.

In relation to the transfer system at the age of eleven (the Eleven Plus), the Commission in 1988 successfully challenged the system of marking, which resulted in young girls having to score higher marks than young boys in order to qualify for a grammar school place. This landmark case resulted in over 800 girls, previously unsuccessful, being given the opportunity of a free grammar school place.

(g)   Sexual Harassment

The position of women at work continues to be undermined by the problem of sexual harassment in the workplace. The value placed on a woman's contribution is damaged by harassment, as is her own self-worth. It is also detrimental to the interests of employers, as it can create an intimidating and uncomfortable environment and can severely affect productivity. The cases brought by the Commission, on behalf of a number of applicants, also show that this kind of unacceptable conduct can attract financial penalties against an employer.

The Commission's publication 'Sexual Harassment is no Laughing Matter' is one of the means of assisting employees, employers, and trade unions to combat sexual harassment in the workplace. It gives examples of sexual harassment and practical advice and steps to take when it is encountered. The publication also details some of the cases brought before the Industrial Tribunals and gives advice to employers and trade union officials.

(h)   Other Areas

Whilst identifying seven priority areas, the Commission also recognises that there are broad policy matters relating to the practice and promotion of equality of opportunity which extend and transcend these seven areas. For example, the Commission has asked the European Commission to examine the provisions in the Fair Employment Act which, in the Commission's view, adversely affect the provisions of the sex discrimination legislation. Other challenges on procedural matters, and to the existing domestic legislation, are under consideration, and the Commission continually keeps the legislation under review and plans to make recommendations for changes and improvements to the sex discrimination legislation.   A Code of Practice is to be prepared and comments are regularly made to Government on legislation and procedures, as appropriate.

STRATEGIES

In all its work to promote equality of opportunity and the elimination of sex discrimination, the Commission employs a variety of strategies.

The strategy which received greatest publicity is that of litigation, and the Commission recently published a casebook setting out the significant cases which have gone before the Northern Ireland Courts and tribunals. This casebook has been distributed to every solicitor's office in Northern Ireland and is in considerable demand from the legal profession, academics, employers, and trade unionists alike.   A shorter version, outlining the twenty most significant cases, is much used by students.

Litigation, however, is not the only strategy available to the Commission; the Commission, under the legislation, has powers to carry out general and formal investigations. These are important means of working towards structural change, primarily in the area of employment, and it is the Commission's intention to have at least one formal investigation under way at any one time.

Encouragement of voluntary compliance with, at the minimum, the obligations of the legislation is an important strategy - one which is relevant pre-litigation, prior to a formal investigation, during litigation or a formal investigation, and at a post-litigation stage. The thrust is for an integrated approach employing negotiation, investigation, or litigation when and as appropriate. What begins as an individual complaint can result in litigation, which may then lead to negotiation with an employer or, if felt appropriate, to an investigation. The aim is for a flexible, integrated approach resulting in maximum benefit and change.

The Commission also sees promotion as an important strategy in providing information on rights and obligations arising out of the legislation. This includes public relations work, lobbying for change, providing advice, and trying to effect voluntary change.

Finally, the Commission's power to assist or commission research provides the factual information which can refute stereotypes and ascertain how inequality between the sexes arises, is maintained, and, in some cases, perpetuated.

SOCIO-ECONOMIC GROUP, GENDER AND REGIONAL INEQUALITIES IN STUDENT PARTICIPATION IN HIGHER EDUCATION

Patrick Clancy

[This paper examines three dimensions of inequality in student participation in higher education in Ireland. The discrepancies that exist between social groups in terms of their representation at University and other third level institutions is explored, together with trends over the time period 1963-1986. The participation of women in higher education, and their representation by field of study, is assessed, along with regional discrepancies in terms of differential county admissions rates to higher education.

Ed.]

The aim of this paper is to provide some data on inequalities in student participation in higher education. Inequalities by socio-economic group, gender and region will be examined. Since my presentation must necessarily be brief, I will not be able to avoid some over-simplification of the issues. My primary objective is descriptive, although some discussion of the policy issues which arise is included. I will start with a consideration of socio-economic group inequalities.

SOCIO-ECONOMIC GROUP

The most recent comprehensive data available on social class inequalities in Irish higher education are contained in my 1988 report WHO GOES TO COLLEGE? This study was based on an analysis of the characteristics of all those who were new entrants to higher education in Autumn 1986. These new entrants constituted 25% of the appropriate age cohort, showing a significant increase on the 20% participation rate recorded from a similar survey of the 1980 intake.

In examining social class differentials in participation, the categories used to measure socio-economic status are those based primarily on occupation, used by the CSO in reporting the Census of Population. While these measures, like many used in social research, are by no means perfect, they enable us to compare the social background of third-level entrants with the relevant section of the national population. Table 1 shows the distribution of 1986 new entrants by socio-economic group together with the 1981 distribution of the national population under the age of 15. The latter is the most appropriate comparative population group for whom data are available since it was from this cohort that the 1988 entrants were drawn. A participation ratio has been calculated showing the degree to which each social group is either proportionately represented, 'over-represented' or 'under-represented' among higher education entrants. Almost 21% of new entrants came from the Farmers social group although this group comprised only 14% of the national population of children in 1981. This gives a participation ratio of 1:45 showing that students from farming backgrounds are 'over-represented' in higher education, having 45% more places than would be anticipated on the basis of their proportionate distribution in the population. Excluding Farmers there are five other socio-economic groups 'over-represented' with a further five 'under-represented'. The most seriously under-represented group (by a factor of six) is that of Unskilled Manual Workers while at the other end of the scale, the Higher Professional group is over-represented by a factor of three.

The results of a similar analysis carried out in respect of 1980 new entrants are also summarised in Table 1, thus enabling us to examine changes in the participation ratio of the different social groups between 1980 and 1986. The pattern of socio-economic disparities is broadly similar in the two studies. In particular the consistency of the findings in respect of the five lower socio-economic groups points to the stubborn persistence of marked social inequalities. The main change over the six year period was the improvement of the position of the Farmers social group at the expense of the five higher socio-economic groups.

While a comparison between the two national surveys in 1980 and 1986 provides an indication of short term trends in socio-economic group inequality, it would be desirable to have the relevant data over a longer period to assess the overall pattern of change. Regrettably the required comprehensive data do not exist. The first data on socio-economic disparities in third-level participation rates dates from the early 1960s. Furthermore, these data are only available for the universities, although at this stage the universities accounted for more than 80% of total higher education enrolments compared to 57% in 1986. Notwithstanding the limitations of the data, Table 2 provides some indication of the pattern of change between 1963 and 1986, a period of far-reaching change in Irish higher education. Data for 1983 are taken from INVESTMENT IN EDUCATION and compared with my 1986 survey data for new entrants to university and for all new entrants. Some of the socio-economic groups shown separately in the more recent report have been combined to conform to the format used in the INVESTMENT IN EDUCATION report.

The overall picture revealed by this comparison is one of consistency rather than one of change; large discrepancies persist between the social groups in their representation at university. The main change over the 25

25

year period is consistent with the short term trend already noted. Farmers who were under-represented in the universities in 1963 had by 1986 13% more places at university than would be justified on the basis of their proportionate size in the population. The rise in the participation rate of the Farmers is compensated for by a decline in the over-representation of the higher socio-economic groups; their participation ratio at university fell from 3.21 in 1963 to 2.27 in 1986. The other three socio-economic categories which were grossly under-represented in 1963 were still seriously under-represented in 1986. While the position of the Semi-skilled and Un-skilled had improved significantly from 0.08 to 0.19 the participation ratio of the Other Non-manual and the Skilled Manual groups had actually declined over the period. When we combine these three categories to calculate a single participation ratio index, the reduction in inequality is very modest: the participation ratio increased from 0.21 to 0.26. Overall it is clear that when we confine our analysis to university entrants only, there is relatively little movement in the direction of equalisation in participation rates. However, the picture is somewhat more optimistic when we look at all new entrants to higher education.

Between 1963 and 1986 total enrolments in full-time education increased by approximately 250%. More significantly, perhaps, this expansion was accompanied by a major structural change and diversification of the system. In the early 1960s higher education outside the university was very limited, consisting mainly of Teacher Training colleges together with a small enrolment in Technological and Professional colleges. The development of the RTCs and the expansion of the existing colleges transformed the structure of opportunity for higher education. By 1986, 56% of new entrants were admitted to colleges outside the university sector. Because of an absence of data it is not possible to monitor changes over the period in the socio-economic background of students in this sector. However it is clear from the differences between the participation ratio of university entrants and all new entrants (Table 2) that the socio-economic group disparities are less marked in the non-university sector.

The differential social selectivity is illustrated in Table 3. Inequality between the social groups is greatest within the university sector; students from the Higher Professional group are most highly represented here while students from working class backgrounds have their lowest representation in this sector. However, there are also large disparities between the social groups in the pattern of enrolment in each of the other sectors. For example, in the RTCs and the DIT, where students from working class backgrounds have their highest representation, the participation ratios reveal considerable disparities. The participation ratio of the five lower socio-economic groups, taken together, was 0.60 in the RTCs and 0.53 in the DIT. In contrast, the participation ratio of the five higher socio-economic groups was 1.27 in the RTCs and 1.94 in the DIT, while the respective ratios for the Farmers group were 1.94 and 0.79. Thus, it is clear than, while all higher education continues to be socially selective, the rapid expansion in the non-university sector has contributed to a reduction in socio-economic group inequalities. The role of the RTCs has been especially significant in this respect.

There is a further aspect of differential selectivity in higher education which is worthy of comment. Within the university sector, the degree of social selectivity varies by field of study. The social reproduction of the middle classes is clearly evident by the disproportionate enrolment of the higher socio-economic groups in the prestigious professional faculties such as Medicine, Veterinary Medicine, Dentistry, Law and Architecture. Thus, the social differentiation by sector is complemented by a further differentiation by field of study within the university sector. I have consciously drawn attention to this differential selectivity, both inter-sector and intra-sector, since it is not often commented upon. We use the single term "higher education" to encompass a highly differentiated phenomenon. It is no accident that the courses in the professional faculties in the universities which are most socially selective tend to be those of longest duration and, hence, have the highest opportunity cost. They also tend to be amongst those courses with the highest points requirement, frequently (at least a third in 1986) necessitating a repeat Leaving Certificate to gain entry. It is clear that the differential social recruitment to these courses is at least partially accounted for by differences in family resources, both economic and cultural.

The documentation of large socio-economic inequalities points to a dilemma for policy makers in higher education both at national and institutional level. The importance of the issue is related to the fact that higher education credentials have increasingly become the passport to high status occupations and financial security. Two different responses are possible. The first is to suggest that the problem and the solution are located elsewhere in the earlier stages of the educational system and in the wider social structure generally. Alternatively it may be that the pattern of provision and the modes of access to higher education may be at least partially responsible.

For those of us involved in higher education it is, of course, easier to suggest that the problem and the solution to socio-economic disparities lie outside higher education. There is much to support this proposition. For example, the only longitudinal study of the Irish education system found that while the social disparities in access to higher education were very pronounced, this was accounted for by selective attrition earlier in the educational system. Greaney & Kellaghan (1984) found that, for their cohort, in the final education transition from Leaving Certificate to higher education in the early 1970s, class was not a significant factor. More recent evidence, from the early 1980s shows that, while there has been a remarkable increase in second level participation with about 70% staying on to take the Leaving Certificate, the drop-out rate remains highly class specific. Furthermore, this very high class differential in retention is complemented by a class differential in level of academic attainment for those who remain (Breen 1986).

It is probable that the genesis of these differences in second level retention and achievement rates is to be found mainly in inequalities in students' family background. In seeking to identify home and family variables which are associated with variation in academic achievement it is now conventional to differentiate between material and economic circumstances of families on the one hand, and cultural and attitudinal features on the other. Thus, unemployment and poverty, the ability to forego earnings however small, the cost of school books uniforms and examination fees, the cost of repeating the Leaving Certificate, housing conditions, the availability of a quiet room in which to study, are all relevant. So also are the attitudes and aspirations of parents and peers, and the kind of cultural climate fostered in the home. In attempting to prioritise the relative importance of these factors most research has pointed to the greater explanatory power of cultural as opposed to material or structural variables. What is frequently forgotten, however, is that the kind of familial cultural orientation which facilitates high educational achievement is itself a function of secure economic and material circumstances. While cultural orientations are not entirely determined by material and structural conditions, they are strongly conditioned by such factors.

While conceding the pre-eminent importance of home and family variables I also believe that the structure of post-primary education contributes to inequality (Clancy 1990). The present system of post-primary education is a highly differentiated one where variations in social selectivity, prestige and academic emphasis range from those found in fee-paying secondary schools through non-fee paying secondary, comprehensive, community and vocational schools. These different school types have, as I have demonstrated (Clancy 1988), different retention rates and different transfer rates to higher education. While it is clear that the differential performance of the various types of schools reflect differences in individual pupil characteristics at intake, it is also certain that the social class composition of the schools has a significant effect on student aspirations and achievement, independent of the social class background of any individual student. The institutionalisation, within a system of publicly funded education, of invidious status hierarchies between different post-primary schools serves to reproduce existing class hierarchies.

How should policy makers in higher education respond to the stark socio-economic group inequalities in participation? They must start with the realisation that a large percentage of the working class have already dropped out of school before the Leaving Certificate. Furthermore of those who take the Leaving Certificate it is probable that their results will be less competitive. An acknowledgement of the latter does not require us to endorse a genetically determined explanation, rather an acceptance of the fact that differential family resources contribute to variation in academic achievement. Two separate sets of policies are needed. The first set must target those who complete the Leaving Certificate and achieve the level of attainment necessary to gain a third level place. For this group the availability and adequacy of financial support becomes critical. In respect of availability, the removal of the four honours requirement for grants, whereby previously some students who gained a college place did not qualify for a grant, is a welcome development. However, the level of financial support is, on its own, not adequate. This is a serious impediment especially for students embarking on a long programme. It is understandable that while many working class students may be happy to embark on a two-year programme of study they are inhibited by the financial implications of a long programme. Thus, the differential social selectivity within higher education will not be eliminated without more generous financial support. I think this should be acknowledged even if we also acknowledge the country's difficult fiscal situation.

A second set of policies will be required to cater for students who, because of family circumstances, do not complete second level and those who are not in a position to go directly to college after leaving school. We need to consciously plan to increase provision for mature students, with conventional matriculation requirements, as a form of second chance education. Much of this demand will need to be met by the expansion of part-time provision. The more widespread adoption of a modular or unitised system would greatly facilitate uptake in this area. The Swedish example suggests that the increased availability of part-time higher education does more to reduce disparities in participation rates between social groups than does the expansion in the number of full-time places. It is safe to assume that when the demographic decline starts to affect higher education at the end of this decade, colleges will find a new zeal for attracting adult students. We will have more credibility if principle rather than expediency dictates our access policy.

GENDER

In contrast to the slow movement towards equalisation of social class representation in higher education, the overall gender disparities in participation have been significantly reduced. However, as the other papers in this conference testify, the position remains problematic in many respects. As recently as the mid-1960s females constituted only 29% of full-time students in higher education. By 1986/87 their representation had increased to 46%. Data on new entrants, available only since 1977, provide the best measure of this continuing trend. In 1977, females constituted 41% of new entrants compared to 48% in 1986. Although increasing at a faster rate than males, it remains an anomaly that females are still in a minority amongst new entrants since they have significantly higher participation rates in the senior cycle of the post-primary sector. In 1986, there was a seven percent differential in favour of females in the final year at second level, compared to four percent differential in favour of males in admission to higher education.

With increasing gender equality in overall participation rates, most interest has shifted to an examination of gender differentials by field of study. Before examining recent data it is useful to view the pattern of change over time, although again this can only be done by limiting our examination to the university sector. Table 4 shows the distribution of full-time university students by gender and field of study in 1950 and 1980 using categories developed by the OECD. In 1950 45% of female students were in the Humanities, with 26% in Medicine and 11.5% in Science. In contrast, 32% of males were in Medicine, with a further 30% in the combined fields of Science and Technology and 29% in a Humanities. Thirty years later, after substantial growth in total enrolment, the distribution of males and females had altered significantly. Science and Technology enrolled 41% of males and 21% of females, while the percentages enrolled in Medicine declined significantly to 12.5% and 11.5% for females.

These data on gender differences in enrolment by field of study are rearranged in the final two columns of Table 4 which show the representation of women in each field of study in 1950 and 1980. This distinction between the representation of women and the distribution of women by field of study, is an important one which is rarely made explicit by researchers. Where the distribution of women by field of study is presented, the universe in question is all female students, the focus being on how they distribute themselves among the different fields of study. When the representation of women in a field of study is presented, the universe in question is all students within a particular field of study, the focus being on the percentage of places taken by women. The use of only one statistic can sometimes give a distorted picture. For example, we note from Table 4 that a higher percentage (11.5%) of females than males (8.2%) enrolled in Science in 1950, while in 1980 a similar percentage (16.7%) of male and female students enroled in Science. Yet we note that the representation of women in Science increased from 36% to 46% over the period. The apparent discrepancy is accounted for by the greater increase in female enrolments over the period. It is clear from Table 4 that the representation of women increased significantly in all fields of study with the exception of Social Sciences & Commerce where it remained constant at 37%. Very large increases in the representation of women occurred in Law (7% to 39%), Science and Technology (14% to 30%) and Medical Sciences (24% to 44%).

The most recent data on the distribution by gender and field of study, of all new entrants to all of higher education are presented in Table 5. These data are taken from the most recent national study (Clancy 1988). The largest percentage (40%) of male new entrants were in the field of technology. In contrast, less that 8% of females were enrolled in Technology, making this the most sex-typed field of study. The largest percentage (24%) of female new entrants enrolled in Commerce, a further 21% entered the Humanities and 16.6% enrolled in Science; the corresponding percentages for males were 21% in Commerce, 13% in Science and 11% in the Humanities. Significantly higher percentages of females enrolled in

Hotel, Catering and Tourism, Social Science, Education and Art and Design, while a much higher percentage of males enrolled in Agriculture. Overall, females constituted the majority in nine of the eleven fields of study. The two exceptions were Technology and Agriculture where females represented less than 15% and 23% of new entrants respectively.

The differentiation by field of study at third level is related to gender differences in subject specialisation at second level. While this latter process has been the subject of a major ESRI study (Hannan and Breen 1983) there has been little analysis of the linkage between both levels, with the exception of one paper which examines the process with respect only to new entrants to the university sector (Clancy and Brannick 1990). Table 6 presents more comprehensive data relating to all new entrants to higher education. It shows, separately for males and females, the average number of Leaving Certificate subjects taken, from each of five different subject groups, by new entrants to the different third-level fields of study. The majority of students present seven subjects for the Leaving Certificate, taking Mathematics, and three languages (Irish, English and French or another modern continental language). The main variability arises in the choice of the three additional subjects. The patterns of choice reflect different propensities to choose from the science group, the business group, the technical group and the heterogeneous "other subjects" group. The overall gender differences in the take-up of Leaving Certificate subjects is shown in the final row of this table: males tend to choose more science, business and technical subjects, while females tend to take more languages and more from the "other subjects" group. However, the most interesting feature of this table is the relationship between subject specialisation at second level and third-level field of study.

Table 6 reveals a clear pattern. Students who take more science subjects at second level are more likely to enter Medicine, Science and Agriculture while those with least science subjects are more likely to enter Art and Design, Hotel, Catering and Tourism, Commerce, the Humanities and Social Science. While there is less variability in the take-up of languages, it is clear that those with more languages enter Law and the Humanities while those with fewer languages· are more likely to enter Art and Design, Technology and Commerce. The pattern of choice with respect to the differential take-up of business subjects is more emphatic. Students who entered Commerce and Hotel, Catering and Tourism had most Leaving Certificate business subjects, while those who entered Medicine had least. The take-up of technical subjects at second level is very low, especially for females, and is associated mainly with those who study technology at third level. The relatively high take-up rate by male education students is accounted for by those who enter Thomond College. Students who enter Art and Design are also more likely to have taken technical subjects. Differential take-up subjects from the "other subjects" group is also linked to third level field of study. Those with more subjects from this group are more likely to enter Art and Design, the Humanities, Hotel, Catering and Tourism, and Social Science.

Having examined the extent of participation of women in higher education and their representation by field of study, I now turn to examine gender differences in the level of study. Again, because of the absence of necessary data, this analysis is confined to HEA designated colleges. Table 7 presents the percentage of degrees earned by women in 1977 and 1987 differentiating by degree level. In addition to differentiating between primary, masters and doctorate degrees, the table also reports the percentage of "upper level" primary degrees. This latter category refers to first class honours, upper division and undifferentiated second class honours degrees. The representation at this level of primary degree is important since it is mainly from this cohort that graduate students are recruited. In 1977 women earned 43% of all primary degrees, however, they were significantly less well represented among those who got "upper level" primary degrees. Their representation was further reduced at masters degree level where they got 24% while at the doctorate level only one fifth of the degrees were earned by women. Comparable data for 1987 show a significant reduction in the gender differential at the higher levels. The percentage of "upper level" primary degrees earned by women is almost equal to the total percentage of primary degrees earned while women earned almost a third of all higher degrees.

The improved participation and performance at primary degree and postgraduate level is highly significant. However there remains a disproportionately high drop-out rate of talented female students, who commence their third level studies with comparable or slightly higher levels of attainment than males.

REGION

The neglect of regional inequalities represents a major lacuna in educational research. In the Irish context this is surprising since this was one of the issues explored in the seminal INVESTMENT IN EDUCATION report. I have addressed this issue in my research on participation. In 1986 the rate of admission to higher education was 25% for the country as a whole. Rates of admission varied significantly by county. Sligo and Kerry shared the highest rates (35%) while, having taken account of students enrolled in Northern Ireland colleges, Dublin and Offaly had the lowest rate of 20%. Dublin's disadvantaged position in Irish higher education is particularly anomalous since it runs directly counter to the situation which prevails in other countries where the larger urban centres tend to have higher levels of participation. The variation in admission rates revealed a distinct regional pattern with higher rates in western counties: six of the nine counties with the lowest rates were from Leinster while the three counties from Ulster made up the remaining three. The geographical disparities revealed are broadly similar to those found by the INVESTMENT IN EDUCATION survey team in the 1960s and in the more recent school leavers surveys (Breen 1984).

In the analysis of correlates of differential county admission rates to higher education two main findings emerge. The first concerns proximity to a third level college, while the second points to the significance of second level retention rates. Distance from a university and distance from a vocational/technological college were negatively associated with the rate of admission to each of these sectors. This finding clearly demonstrates the regional impact of the locational policy of the RTCs. However, the research findings also suggest that in our analysis we need to differentiate between different sectors of higher education, since accessibility to different forms of higher education influences the number of students enrolling in each sector. The evidence suggests that high rates of admission to technological education (i.e. the mainly short cycle sector) in many counties may be influenced as much by the distance from a university centre as by the proximity of a technological college. Thus, the structure of opportunity in a region is shaped by the type and range of third level facilities which are accessible.

The second major finding was that retention rate to Leaving Certificate was a predictor of the rate of admission to higher education. Counties with low rates of admission to higher education tended to have low retention rates at second level. Dublin was the county with the lowest retention rate, suggesting that part of the problem of low third-level admission is located in the high drop-out rate at second level. Hence, while the decision to proceed with the building of the new RTC at Tallaght will help to address one of the problems in the Dublin area viz., the scarcity of short-cycle places, it needs to be supplemented by initiatives at second level which counteract the highly class specific early drop-out rates at second level.

CONCLUSION

For clarity of presentation I have examined separately three dimensions of inequality in student participation in higher education. In reality, of course, the three dimensions overlap in structuring access to higher education. The interaction between region and social class is perhaps most obvious. There is considerable variation between counties in the degree of socio-economic group inequalities in participation. Significantly, Dublin's lowest participation rate is matched by its having the highest score on a socio-economic group inequality index. Furthermore, an earlier study (Clancy and Benson 1979) had shown that the striking differential participation rates for different parts of the city and county reflect the socio-economic group paterning of the population. Finally, it is of interest to note the interaction between class and gender disparities of participation (Table 8). Females from working class backgrounds are the most under-represented group in higher education: for each of the lower socio-economic groups, the participation ratio is even lower for females than it is for males. In contrast, females from the Farmers social group have a significantly higher participation ratio (1.66) than males (1.22). This latter gender differential may be related to the pattern of male inheritance, making males less dependent on education to secure future status. These socio-economic group and gender differentials point to the complex interaction between structural and cultural forces which give rise to these differentials. Unfortunately, in the current state of our knowledge it remains easier to describe than to explain these disparities.

BIBLIOGRAPHY

Breen, R.   EDUCATION AND THE LABOUR MARKET, Dublin, ESRI, 1984.

Breen, R.   SUBJECT AVAILABILITY AND STUDENT PERFORMANCE IN THE SENIOR CYCLE OF IRISH POST-PRIMARY SCHOOLS, Dublin, ESRI, 1986.

Clancy, P. WHO GOES TO COLLEGE? Dublin, HEA, 1988.

Clancy, P. "Selection for College: some implications for second level" COMPASS, Vol. 11, (1990), (in press).

Clancy, P. and Benson, C.   HIGHER EDUCATION IN DUBLIN: A STUDY OF SOME EMERGING NEEDS, Dublin, HEA, 1979.

Clancy, P. and Brannick, T.   "Subject specialisation at second level and third level field of study".   IRISH EDUCATION STUDIES, Vol. 9, (1990).

Greaney, V. and Kellaghan, T. EQUALITY OF OPPORTUNITY IN IRISH SCHOOLS, Dublin, The Education Co., 1984.

Hannan, D.R., Breen, R. *et al.* SCHOOLING AND SEX ROLES, Dublin, ESRI, 1983.

TABLE 1

SOCIO-ECONOMIC STATUS OF 1986 ENTRANTS TO HIGHER EDUCATION AND
NATIONAL POPULATION UNDER 15 YRS IN 1981 WITH PARTICIPATION RATIOS
BY SOCIO-ECONOMIC GROUP FOR 1986 AND 1980

Socio-Economic Groups	Higher Education Entrants in 1986 %	National Population Under 15 yrs in 1981 %	Participation Ratio 1986	Participation Ratio 1980
Farmers	20.8	14.3	1.45	1.04
Other Agricultural Occupations	1.4	2.9	0.48	0.21
Higher Professional	12.0	4.0	3.00	3.93
Lower Professional	9.2	4.3	2.14	2.29
Employers & Managers	18.2(15.8)*	9.2	1.98(1.72)*	2.75
Salaried Employees	6.2	2.7	2.30	2.93
Intermediate Non-Manual Workers	9.8(12.3)*	10.2	0.96(1.21)*	1.11
Other Non-Manual Workers	5.7	12.8	0.45	0.50
Skilled Manual Workers	12.9	25.4	0.51	0.51
Semi-Skilled Manual Workers	2.5	5.9	0.42	0.49
Unskilled Manual Workers	1.3	8.2	0.16	0.11
TOTAL %	100.0	100.0		
N	14,388	969,951		

* These percentages and participation ratios have been adjusted to take account of
   possible bias in classification of certain occupations (see text for details).

TABLE 2.

PARTICIPATION RATIO OF SOCIO-ECONONIC GROUPS AMONG NEW
ENTRANTS TO HIGHER EDUCATION 1963 AND 1986

SOCIO-ECONOMIC GROUPS	UNIVERSITY ENTRANTS		ALL THIRD LEVEL ENTRANTS
	1963	1986	1986
Farmers	0.79	1.13	1.45
Professsional/Managerial/			
Intermediate Non-manual	3.21	2.27	1.82
Other non-manual	0.30	0.27	0.50
Skilled Manual	0.40	0.31	0.51
Semi-skilled/Unskilled			
Manual	0.08	0.19	0.30

41

TABLE 3

SOCIO-ECONOMIC STATUS OF NEW ENTRANTS TO HIGHER EDUCATION IN 1986, BY COLLEGE TYPE

Socio-Economic Groups	Univ. %	NIHE %	DIT %	RTC %	Colls of Ed %	Other Colls %	Total %
Farmers	16.2	23.7	11.3	27.8	32.1	7.6	20.3
Other Agricultural Occupations	0.9	1.8	1.4	1.9	1.2	1.0	1.4
Higher Professional	19.0	9.1	11.7	5.7	4.1	18.3	12.0
Lower Professional	11.0	10.1	7.4	6.5	14.1	13.6	9.2
Employers & Managers	17.9	14.8	26.4	15.9	17.1	26.2	18.2
Salaried Employees	8.1	9.0	6.0	3.9	3.9	7.3	6.2
Intermediate Non-Manual Workers	13.1	12.5	7.7	6.9	8.5	5.3	9.3
Other Non-Manual Workers	3.5	4.6	8.5	7.6	4.8	6.0	5.7
Skilled Manual Workers	8.0	10.5	16.3	17.9	11.1	12.3	12.9
Semi-Skilled Manual Workers	2.1	3.4	1.9	3.0	2.2	2.3	2.5
Unskilled Manual Workers	0.3	0.5	1.3	2.9	0.9	0.0	0.3
TOTAL %	100.0	100.0	100.0	100.0	100.0	100.0	100.0
TOTAL N	5,512	1,016	1,803	4,900	856	301	14.388

TABLE 4

DISTRIBUTION OF FULL-TIME UNIVERSITY STUDENTS BY FIELD OF STUDY AND GENDER AND REPRESENTATION OF WOMEN 1950 AND 1980

	1950		1980		Representation of women	
	Female %	Male %	Female %	Male %	1950 %	1980 %
Science	11.5	8.2	16.7	16.7	36	46
Technology	0.0	12.8	2.0	16.8	0	9
Architecture	1.0	2.6	0.7	1.1	14	36
Agriculture & Veterinary Med.	0.1	6.0	1.7	6.7	1	18
Sub-Total Science & Technology	12.6	29.5	21.2	41.4	14	30
Medical Sciences	25.7	31.9	11.5	12.5	24	44
Humanities	44.7	29.2	40.7	21.7	38	61
Education	8.6	2.9	12.5	4.5	54	70
Law	0.2	1.1	3.3	4.4	7	39
Social Sciences & Commerce	8.1	5.4	10.8	15.5	37	37
Total %	100	100	100	100	28	46
N	1,932	4,940	10,617	12,600	-	-

43

TABLE 5

DISTRIBUTION OF ALL NEW ENTRANTS TO HIGHER EDUCATION BY GENDER AND REPRESENTATION OF WOMEN WITHIN EACH FIELD OF STUDY IN 1986

	Males %	Females %	Total N	Total %	Representation of women %
Humanities	10.9	21.2	2,720	15.9	63.9
Art & Design	2.4	5.7	683	4.0	67.9
Science	12.9	16.6	2,531	14.8	54.2
Agriculture	2.3	0.7	265	1.5	23.0
Technology	40.4	7.6	4,240	24.7	14.7
Medical Sciences	3.2	4.1	626	3.7	53.8
Education	2.8	8.1	916	5.3	72.6
Law	1.4	1.8	273	1.6	53.5
Social Science	1.8	5.9	639	3.7	75.0
Commerce	20.7	24.0	3,817	22.3	51.5
Hotel, Catering & Tourism	1.2	4.2	449	2.6	76.8
Total %	100.0	100.0	-	100.0	47.8
N	8,964	8,195	17,159	-	-

TABLE 6

AVERAGE NUMBER OF SCIENCE, LANGUAGE, BUSINESS, TECHNICAL AND "OTHER" SUBJECTS TAKEN AT LEAVING CERTIFICATE BY THIRD LEVEL FIELD OF STUDY AND GENDER

FIELD OF STUDY	Science Subjects		Language Subjects		Business Subjects		Other Subjects		Technical Subjects	
	M	F	M	F	M	F	M	F	M	F
Humanities	1.10	1.09	3.05	3.15	0.93	0.50	1.39	1.60	0.09	0.00
Art & Design	0.79	0.73	2.33	2.81	0.57	0.42	1.94	2.10	0.46	0.03
Social Science	1.08	1.17	2.89	3.09	0.94	0.48	1.12	1.45	0.21	0.01
Education	1.15	1.24	2.79	3.05	0.49	0.44	0.87	1.36	0.82	0.01
Law	1.52	1.43	3.18	3.17	0.61	0.43	0.98	1.24	0.11	0.00
Hotel, Catering & Tourism	1.01	0.80	2.87	2.93	1.01	0.89	1.34	1.59	0.08	0.00
Commerce	0.99	0.96	2.76	2.92	1.42	1.00	0.95	1.24	0.12	0.01
Medical Science	2.65	2.22	2.78	3.10	0.23	0.22	0.53	0.83	0.06	0.00
Science	2.05	1.85	2.84	3.02	0.43	0.37	0.84	1.08	0.19	0.01
Agriculture	1.91	1.83	2.96	3.09	0.57	0.40	0.86	1.11	0.19	0.00
Technology	1.47	1.41	2.54	2.86	0.56	0.63	0.83	1.23	0.70	0.04
Total	1.41	1.25	2.72	2.99	0.76	0.60	0.95	1.35	0.39	0.01

TABLE 7

PERCENTAGE OF DEGREES EARNED BY WOMEN IN HEA-DESIGNATED
INSTITUTIONS, BY DEGREE LEVEL IN 1977 AND 1987

DEGREE LEVEL	1977	1987
Primary degree (total)	43	45
First, Upper Second or Undifferentiated		
Second	31	43
Master Degree	24	33
Doctorate	20	32

TABLE 8

PERCENTAGE DISTRIBUTION & PARTICIPATION RATIO OF NEW ENTRANTS TO
HIGHER EDUCATION BY SOCIO-ECONOMIC STATUS AND GENDER

Socio-Economic Groups	Male %	Female %	Male %	Female %
Farmers	71.5	23.8	1.22	1.66.
Other Agricultural Occupations				
Higher Professional	1.4	1.3	0.48	0.45
Lower Professional	12.7	11.8	3.18	2.95
Employers & Managers	9.1	9.5	2.12	2.21
Salaried Employees	18.5	18.2	2.01	1.98
Intermediate Non-Manual	6.7	5.6	2.48	2.07
Workers				
Other Non-Manual Workers	10.6	9.0	1.04	0.38
Skilled Manual Workers	5.8	5.6	0.45	0.44
Semi-Skilled Manual Workers	13.6	11.8	0.54	0.46
Unskilled Manual Workers	2.7	2.2	0.46	0.37
	1.5	1.2	0.18	0.15
TOTAL %	100.0	100.0		
TOTAL N	8,964	8,196		

GENDER EQUALITY IN THE CURRICULUM IN SECOND LEVEL SCHOOLS

Catherine Fitzpatrick

[This paper addresses the issue of equality of opportunity in Second Level schools, and the role of the Association of Secondary Teachers in Ireland in the provision of gender equality in the schools and the curriculum.

Ed.]

INTRODUCTION

The Association of Secondary Teachers in Ireland (A.S.T.I.) is the major union representing teachers in second-level education. Being both a trade union and a professional organisation for teachers, the A.S.T.I. is one of the major voices in Irish education. The issue of equality has emerged as one of the major concerns of the union in recent years. This is evidenced in the establishment of an Equality Committee at Annual Convention 1988. Specific responsibility for equality matters has been assigned to the Industrial Relations Officer. The equality policy of the A.S.T.I. focuses on three main areas:-

- Members' working conditions.
- Equality of opportunity within the union.
- Equality of opportunity between the sexes within schools and in the curriculum.

In this paper I will outline the role of the A.S.T.I. in the promotion of gender equality in schools and in the curriculum. I will also refer to the possible impact of this policy on the choices pupils make when they proceed to third level education. In formulating an equality policy aimed at achieving equality of opportunity between the sexes within schools and in the curriculum, the A.S.T.I. clearly stated the objective of this policy:

- The establishment of a type of organisation and curriculum in the schools which affords male and female pupils equal opportunities in terms of subject options, academic achievement and future training/educational and career choices.

The realisation of this objective will be pursued as follows:

- The A.S.T.I. will urge the Department of Education to initiate and support the introduction of equality interventions in all second-level schools.

- Teacher training authorities and responsible educational bodies will be requested to facilitate the promotion of equality of opportunity between the sexes in the curriculum and in their training programmes and recommendations.

- A.S.T.I. members will be requested to actively promote equality of opportunity within their own schools.

Having defined the policy objectives, the A.S.T.I. Equality Committee then considered the most effective strategies to promote and implement the equality policy. It was decided to concentrate on the following:

- The School.
- The Branch.
- Education policy at national level.

THE SCHOOL

The A.S.T.I. believes that the promotion of gender equality is the responsibility of all members in all schools. School Stewards are asked to promote the equality policy within the schools. However, the Equality Committee recognised that to effectively promote equality in schools and in the curriculum, schools would require guidelines. Guidelines were drafted after the Equality Committee had undertaken a review of research on the subject of equality in schools and in the curriculum, and had consulted some of the reports/recommendations which have issued in recent years from institutions in Ireland and from the European Commission. The following guidelines were issued to all School Stewards:-

- the curriculum range and organisation of subjects on offer should provide for equality of opportunity between male and female pupils;

- the school should encourage the uptake of non-traditional subjects by the under-represented gender and should ensure that traditional subjects are not set against each other; periodic reviews of progress in this area should be undertaken;

- staffs should consider strategies to promote gender equality in the school, including an examination of the following items:
  - attitudes of staff,
  - attitudes of parents,
  - school ethos,
  - teaching materials used,

- sexism in the curriculum
  (focus on women's contributions and achievements in literature, science, technology and history),
- intervention for parents,
- intervention for pupils,
  (including a specific module on gender equality).

- the formulation of a school policy on sex equity and anti-sexism is desirable;

- some staff in-service days should be devoted to training in the promotion of gender equality

THE BRANCH

In order to promote the A.S.T.I. equality policy at branch level, the A.S.T.I. Equality Committee recommended that branches establish Equality Networks (of two to four members). A training course is organised for members of the equality networks. The A.S.T.I. equality policy is discussed and strategies to implement same are suggested.

The Equality Networks fulfil several important functions:

- Assist branch officers in the promotion, implementation and monitoring of A.S.T.I. equality policy;

- Advise and assist members in schools;

- Liaise with and report to the Equality Committee;

- Ensure that equality is an item on the agenda for branch meetings;

- Submit motions on equality issues to Annual Convention.

To date 11 branches have established Equality Networks and several have indicated their intention to do so. The A.S.T.I. Equality Committee believes that the Equality Networks have an important role to play in raising the level of awareness among members about equality issues.

EDUCATIONAL POLICY AT NATIONAL LEVEL

A.S.T.I. Equality Policy at national level is pursued through:

- Negotiations with the Department of Education.
- Negotiations with management organisations.
- Submission of motions to I.C.T.U. Annual Congress.

The A.S.T.I. has identified the following issues as being crucial in achieving equality of opportunity within the curriculum:

Subject Provision

The A.S.T.I. seeks to ensure that all pupils have equal access to all available subjects. Subject choice at second level has a major impact on pupils' future education opportunities at third level and future career options. The low uptake among girls of the Physical Sciences, Higher

Maths and Technical subjects is of particular concern. There has been increased provision for girls in the Physical Sciences and Higher Maths in recent years and this has resulted in increased uptake. However, many girls' schools do not have adequate science laboratory facilities to offer science as an option for all pupils in the junior cycle. Consequently a significant number of girls do not take Science at Junior cycle and thus are effectively prevented from choosing science subjects in the Senior cycle. The A.S.T.I. carried out a survey on the provision for teaching of science subjects in second level schools in 1987/'88. The result revealed that the percentages of single-sex girls schools with all Junior classes taking science is much lower than single-sex boys schools. Out of a total of 97 single-sex boys' schools, in 86 schools, all students took Junior Science. However, out of 113 single-sex girls schools, only 36 schools had all students taking science at Junior Cycle Level. Despite the improvement in uptake of Higher Maths and Science at junior cycle, girls are still very under-represented in these subjects at Senior cycle level. There is clearly a need for intervention projects to remedy this situation and there has been some progress in this area. The Department of Education initiated intervention projects in physics and chemistry in 1985, with the aim of increasing the number of girls studying these subjects. These projects have been very successful and the A.S.T.I. is seeking to have these intervention projects extended to more schools. The majority of single-sex girls schools do not provide Technical subjects, as traditionally Technical subjects have been perceived as "boys'" subjects. Thus girls are deprived of the opportunity to develop the skills, confidence and foundation which would enable them to pursue a wide range of technological courses at third level. The A.S.T.I. believes that this inequality needs to be addressed urgently. Even if Third Level Colleges do not require girls to have studied a Science or Technical subject for admission to Science, Engineering and Technology courses, girls are at a distinct disadvantage when they embark on these courses. The A.S.T.I. believes that this issue should be addressed through:

- Action Research on Girls and Technology
- Pilot intervention projects in Technology.

Subject Allocation

Research has shown that subject provision does not necessarily result in access to a subject. Co-educational schools initially make provision for both boys and girls. However in practice many co-educational schools operate allocation procedures which result in boys being given priority in Science and Technical subjects and girls in Languages, Commerce and Home Economics. Some schools operate exclusionary rules, allocating traditional subjects to boys and girls. In these schools it is usual practice to timetable Technical and Science subjects against Home Economics, Commerce, Art and Music. This significantly reduces the probability of girls or boys choosing a non-traditional subject as research has shown that in this situation girls and boys will opt for what they perceive to be the most gender appropriate subject. A.S.T.I. policy in this area is very clear:

"The organisation of the curriculum in the school should be such as to facilitate equal access to all available subjects."

The A.S.T.I. will seek to have training on this issue provided for Principals, Vice-Principals and Guidance Counsellors.

TEACHER TRAINING

The A.S.T.I. believes that pre-service and in-service training for teachers on the issue of gender equality is vital, if progress is to be made in promoting and achieving gender equality in second-level schools. Research indicates that teachers' attitude have a significant effect on pupils' attitudes and expectations. Consequently teachers who hold stereotypical views on gender are very likely to convey them to their pupils. Research has shown that even when there is equal provision for and access to subjects in the curriculum, pupils' attitudes play a significant role in maintaining the traditional pattern of uptake in subjects. Teacher training on this issue should include:

-       instruction on the nature, extent and effect of gender stereotyping in education and society,

-       an analysis of practices designed to combat sex stereotyping.

The A.S.T.I. will seek to have a module on gender equality included in pre-service training programmes for all subject areas.

SEX STEREOTYPING IN TEXTBOOKS AND TEACHING MATERIALS.

Sex stereotyping in textbooks and teaching materials reinforces the existing blueprint which pupils have about gender appropriate roles. The A.S.T.I. will seek the agreement of the Department of Education to urge publishers to confer with teacher bodies prior to publication of new texts. Sexism in textbooks and teaching materials should be monitored. It should be identified, examined and redressed where it arises. The A.S.T.I. welcomes the Minister for Education's recent initiative in this area. A working-group, representative of the Department, school management bodies, teacher unions and the National Parents Council, has been established to examine the position in regard to sexism in textbooks and teaching materials at second-level and to make recommendations on the matter. The A.S.T.I. Equality Committee is presently drawing up a module on gender equality to be included as an element in the civics and political studies course and as an element in either Junior English, Transition Year Option, Vocational Preparation Training Programme or History.

TEACHER APPOINTMENT/ APPOINTMENT TO PRINCIPALSHIP

Teachers are important role models for their pupils and it would be undesirable if teachers were perceived by pupils to undertake stereotypical roles. The A.S.T.I. will urge schools to employ a more equal distribution of male and female teachers across the subject options. The recent appointments to Principalships are also being monitored by the A.S.T.I. Equality Committee. There is an imbalance between the number of potential female appointees (62% of A.S.T.I. members are female) and the appointment of women teachers to principalships. In 1989/90 only 18% of appointments were female. There is also concern that women are not being appointed to single-sex boys schools and they are less likely to be appointed to a co-educational school. Consequently pupils will be confronted with few models of women in positions of authority and power and thus will be more likely to expect men to occupy positions of leadership. A recent A.S.T.I. survey demonstrated that there is a hesitancy on the part of female teachers to apply for principalships, and a survey will be undertaken to determine what factors might deter women teachers from competing for principalships.

CAREER GUIDANCE

Career guidance counsellors play a key role in advising on subject and career choice and it is essential that the training of career guidance counsellors includes instruction on gender equality. They have a very important role to play in interventions with subject teachers parents and pupils to encourage pupils to choose careers which match their abilities and interests regardless of gender. The A.S.T.I. will seek to ensure that all schools have access to a Career Guidance Counselling service. This year the A.S.T.I. Equality Committee, in an effort to encourage second-level students to consider alternative careers, organised an essay competition in conjunction with the Construction Industry Federation. The essay was promoted by Career Guidance Counsellors and English teachers and School Stewards and the response rate was good. This is just one example of an initiative which helps to raise the level of awareness of gender equality in schools.

RATIONALISATION

Declining pupil numbers at second level will result in the rationalisation of small schools into one unit. This will result in fewer single-sex schools. There is some concern that this might have an adverse effect on girls' education and that co-education could reinforce sex stereotyping. The A.S.T.I. will encourage all schools to formulate an equality policy so that all pupils have equality of opportunity in education.

GENDER EQUALITY AND THE RELATIONSHIP BETWEEN SECOND LEVEL EDUCATION AND THIRD LEVEL EDUCATION.

As I have outlined, the A.S.T.I. is actively involved in addressing the issue of gender equality in education and in promoting same. The achievement of gender equality will take some time and will require resources. As initiatives begin to impact, pupils will be challenged to question their traditional sex stereotyped views on gender appropriate roles and careers. This should result in a more equal distribution of boys and girls in the uptake of subjects. When these pupils proceed to Third Level Education there should also be a more equal distribution of male and female students in the uptake of courses. If a gender equality policy can be implemented at second level, girls in particular will benefit in terms of course options at Third Level and future career choices. In the long term gender equality policy should result in an increased number of girls opting for Science, Technology and Engineering Courses because they will have acquired the skill, confidence and a foundation in these subjects at second level, to enable them to further their studies at Third Level. This however will be a slow process. The curriculum, including the hidden curriculum must encourage pupils to question and challenge traditional notions about gender appropriate roles and careers. Equality is now becoming an issue in second level schools but much work and research needs to be done on this issue. The A.S.T.I. notes and welcomes the Minister for Education's initiative on equality in schools when she launched an equality pack on "Gender Equality in Schools" last year. The A.S.T.I. is committed to achieving gender equality in education and will support initiatives on this issue.

EQUAL OPPORTUNITIES:
QUEEN'S UNIVERSITY BELFAST

Stuart Spence

[This paper explores the manner in which the provision of equal opportunity has been addressed in Queen's University Belfast, and its experience to date.

Ed.]

The Queen's University of Belfast was originally established as Queen's College Belfast in 1845. The Act which set up the University prohibited any preference for any religious denomination. Under the 1908 Irish University Act the Queen's College of Belfast was established as a separate University, the Queen's University of Belfast, and the principle of non-discrimination was preserved. The Policy of the University, based on the principle of equality of opportunity enshrined in its Charter since 1908, is to ensure that no person by reason of religious belief, political opinion, sex, marital status, race, colour, ethnic origin or disability is treated less favourably or is disadvantaged for those reasons, by conditions or requirements which cannot be justified. This principle applies both to applicants for employment, and to employees, with respect to advancement, promotion, transfer, training, benefits, facilities, procedures and all other terms and conditions of employment. The University has been, and will continue to be, committed to implementing policies designed to promote equality of opportunity and to absolutely reject unlawful discrimination of any kind.

During and after the Second World War, there was a marked increase in student numbers: between 1938 and 1964 the student population rose from 1,600 to 4,100. The present student population is around 6,500. There are around 2,500 members of staff.

In May 1986, the University's Personnel Officer was designated as its Equal Opportunities Officer. In September 1986 the Fair Employment Agency (FEA) decided to conduct a formal investigation into the provision of equality of opportunity by QUB. This investigation was part of a broader review of equality of opportunity in the province's higher education system.

Also in September 1986, the University's Senate reiterated 'its commitment to fair employment and agreed to set up an Equal Opportunities Group comprising two Pro-Vice-Chancellors, the Honorary Treasurer and the Personnel Officer as Equal Opportunities Officer. In June 1988 a member of the academic staff, who was seconded part-time to supervise the setting up of a monitoring procedure, joined the Equal Opportunities Group. In September 1988, an Equal Opportunities Unit was established and a Clerical Officer appointed. The Unit presently comprises an Administration Officer, appointed in April 1990, and a Clerical Officer, appointed in March 1990.

The University began monitoring its staff in 1988. The University also undertook to monitor its applicant flow.

At the end of January 1989, the monitoring of staff in post had been completed. Around this time, the FEA published the report of their investigation. During the course of the investigation the University had sought to develop its Equal Opportunities Programme through both the establishment of the Equal Opportunities Unit and through its involvement with the Department of Economic Development in the Fair Employment Support Scheme.

Under the Scheme, the University agreed an Action Plan. Some of the main features were:-

(a)   Revision of the Equal Opportunities Policy.

(b)   A review of selection procedures for all employee groupings.

(c)   Word of mouth recruitment declared impermissible.

(d)   Care taken in newspaper advertisement to ensure that all sections of the community are reached.

(e)   All interviewers to be instructed in the essentials of an effective and unbiased interview.

(f)   The establishment of a system to monitor recruitment, promotion, training and termination of employment.

Following the publication of the FEA report, the University agreed to incorporate a number of measures into an updated Equal Opportunities Statement.   This Statement has been approved by the University and is currently with the Trade Unions for comment.   In detail, the University agreed the following Programme of Action with the FEA:-

(a)   QUB will appoint a full-time Officer with day-to-day responsibility for Equal Opportunities who will develop, co-ordinate and monitor the effectiveness of that Policy.

(b)   The University will review recruitment practice, particularly in relation to advertising, so that vacancies will be advertised publicly in such a manner as to ensure that they reach all potential candidates. The University will also ensure that candidates from any under-represented community can recognise that vacancies apply to them and that, where appropriate, consideration will be given to the inclusion of a statement in advertisements that applications are particularly welcome from Catholics. (QUB will also be considering the appropriateness of including statements that encourage female applications where appropriate).

(c)   QUB will review the Equal Opportunities implications of internal promotion procedures and if need be, open up senior vacancies to outside competition in order to widen the pool of applicants.

(d)   QUB will contact all local schools with a view to drawing up a programme to inform school leavers of the type of employment opportunities which may arise within the campus.

(e)   Finally, QUB undertook to conduct a detailed analysis of recent monitoring of current employees and of applicants for posts, and affirmative action taken to attempt to remedy any under-representation.

What we have in the DED and FEA Action Plans are general and obvious steps which all organisations should take on the road to provision of equality of opportunity. The implementation of such action is not necessarily dependent upon monitoring and the analysis of the information obtained.

However, monitoring provides the essential information to ascertain if an organisation is providing equality of opportunity. It provides the basic information on which an Affirmation Action Programme can be established.

Michael Pearn of Pearn Kandola Downs has said that a better understanding of monitoring is achieved by reference to what he calls the Medical Model of Monitoring. He sees monitoring as having three distinct aspects. They are:-

1.   Monitoring as a health check-up -
     Typically it answers such questions as:
     -      Is my organisation in a healthy state?
     -      Is everything working as it should?
     -      Are there symptoms of concern?

2.   Monitoring as diagnosis -
     Typical questions are:
     -      What is causing that symptom?
     -      What is wrong in that situation?
     -      What remedies are open to me?

3.   Monitoring as prognosis -
     Typical questions are:
     -      What will happen over a period of time if nothing
            is done?
     -      How long will it be before the situation becomes
            more serious?
     -      How long will it take to recover?
     -      What can we reasonably expect to happen over
            the   next x months/years?

In summary, monitoring plays a crucial role in assessing the status quo; identifying the need for change and the extent of that change, formulating achievable, specific and measurable goals, and setting them against realistic timetables; measuring progress towards the achievement of those goals; helping the organisation to understand why less than expected progress is being made; and ultimately identifying when those goals have been achieved.

In analysing monitoring information, it is important to avoid complex statistical analysis - again to quote Michael Pearn:

"At one level it is merely a question of examining the figures and simple percentages and asking are there fewer or more than we would reasonably expect under the circumstances. More complex statistical analysis, and some form of manpower modelling or forecasting may be required to identify realistically achievable goals and targets."

Nonetheless, the preliminary analysis should be done by people who have the best understanding of how the organisation actually works. Personnel Managers or Equal Opportunities Advisors get better results when analysis and interpretation is done collaboratively.

What should be done with the data obtained from monitoring? - Ask more questions. Typically the range of questions that are and can be asked include:

1.   Is there an imbalance between what we find and what we would reasonably expect?

2.   Is there an equitable distribution between people from different communities or between the sexes?

3.   Is there fair participation?

4.   Are some people under-represented or over-represented? Can we explain this?

5.   Are some people under-utilised in terms of their potential and skill within the organisation? Can we explain this? Can we tolerate it?

6.   Are there differences in the rates at which we select/promote/transfer/give access to benefits, etc.?

7.   Is there inconsistency between departments? Can it be explained or justified?

8.   Is there discrimination occurring here?

9.   Is what we find fair?

The EOC booklet - "Making Change for Women at Work" -provides excellent guidance on the implementation of an Equal Opportunities Programme and in particular gives an indication of the type of statistics which should be collected, and also some of the questions which should be considered in their analysis.   On the basis of this analysis problems can be identified and the necessary positive action measures can be planned.

The planning of affirmative action should be pro-active, long-term, incremental, strategic, evaluative, and results orientated.

In general, questions about fairness and discrimination are very hard to answer based solely on statistical data.   Consequently, the notion of fair participation is quite a difficult one to answer.   On the other hand, when rephrased as, "'Is there an imbalance here?" or "Are there fewer than we might reasonably expect under the circumstances?", the answer is more of a descriptive nature than an evaluative nature. Consequently, questions that refer to imbalance, uneven distributions, under-representation and under-utilisation, inconsistency and differences in rates, are more easily addressed as the key questions to be answered.

The University recently provided its first monitoring return under the 1989 Fair Employment Act. The Act requires breakdown of staff by occupational classification, religion and sex.

It is the intention of the Equal Opportunities Unit to identify from the monitoring information (both for current staff and for applicants) where there are areas of concern. Once these areas have been identified, in-depth analysis will be conducted into that particular area with a view to identifying the problems and designing appropriate remedial action. It was decided that the first occupational group to be subjected to in-depth analysis should be the academic grades.

During work on this analysis, it became apparent that a proper examination of the position of female academics must cover at least the following areas:-
(a)   current position
(b)   applicant flow
(c)   length of service
(d)   promotion rates
(e)   age
(f)   wastage.

A SUMARY OF WORK TO DATE ON THE ANALYSIS ON THE ANALYSIS OF ACADEMIC STAFF AT QUEEN'S UNIVERSITY, BELFAST

Current Position

Males are disproportionately represented, totalling around 88% of academic staff. Female staff are concentrated in the Lecturer A/B categories - 30% of Lecturers Grade A are female as opposed to only 5% female representation amongst the Senior Lecturers.

These figures correspond to the position of female academics in other British Universities, as outlined in Vernon Bogdanor's article in the Times Higher Educational Supplement (1990, February 2).

Female student representation varies between faculties and it is only to be expected that this be reflected in the breakdown of academic staff by faculty. Female representation varies between 32% in Law to only 2% in Engineering.

It will be noted that the above data exclude Agriculture and Food Science, Clinical and Part-time staff.

Between 1975 and 1988 the proportion of women studying in British Universities increased from 35% to 42%. In 1988/89 the proportion studying in QUB was 43.5%, and varied from 11.3% studying in the Faculty of Engineering to 58% in Arts. (These data include all part-time and full-time undergraduates and postgraduates.) The comparison of female student representation with female academic representation by faculty, is a useful indicator to show what level of participation by women one could reasonably expect.

Applicant Flow

The work to date would seem to indicate that females are being appointed in greater proportion to the level of applications, than are males. There are, however, immediately identifiable areas where the rate of applications from females is lower than what could be expected, having regard to the number of female students studying in the relevant fields. While female application levels remain low, the marginally superior appointment rate for females, even if it is sustained, will not affect the overall representation of females in these areas to any significant degree in the near future.

Length of Service

Around 44% of current female academics joined the University since 1982, as compared to 22% of male staff. Only 8.3% of the male staff joined the University since 1987 while 27.9% of female staff joined in that period.

Of staff appointed since 1987, 31% have been female; whilst this is less than might be expected the above data show a trend of increasing representation for women amongst the academic staff. This trend must be continued and if possible expedited. It is also essential that the increase of women in the Lecturer A/B Grades be shadowed by an increase in representation at more senior grades. It is clear, then, that an analysis of promotion rates is required to identify whether this can be predicted.

Promotion

It must be noted that in practice promotion from lecturer A to lecturer B occurs when the candidate has achieved the final salary point on the lecturer A scale. No formal application for promotion is required once this point has been reached and consideration for promotion is automatic. It must further be noted that promotions from lecturer to senior lecturer consist of both individual applications and also recommendation from Heads of Departments.

Of a total of 430 staff appointed pre 1982, 62% have been promoted. 63% of males have been promoted and 53% of females have been promoted.

Of a total of 141 staff appointed post 1981, 19% have been promoted. 10% of females have been promoted and 22% of males have been promoted.

Age

An analysis of age breakdown amongst academic staff shows that 55% of female staff are below 40 years of age compared to 29% of male staff. 6% of female staff are 50 years or over compared to 30% of male staff.

25% of female staff below 40 years of age have been promoted as compared to 37% of males in that category. 47% of female staff above 40 years of age have been promoted as compared to 61% of males in that category.

It is encouraging that a large percentage of female staff are under 40 years of age, and this reflects the increasing representation of women in recent years. However, it is clear that the promotion rate for women is lower than that for men. If this trend continues, the increasing representation of (young) women will not result in a proportionately balanced representation at senior levels in the near future, although the fact that female representation is increasing will result in a better balance than at present. It is interesting that 53% of female academics below 40 years of age are in the lecturer A/B category as compared to 26% of males.

An analysis of the 1989 promotion exercise shows that 69 candidates were considered for promotion from Lecturer to Senior Lecturer - 5 females and 64 males. 12 males were successful (19% of males considered) and no females were successful. Women in this category amounted to 7% of the total considered, and males amounted to 93% of the total. 9% of female Lecturers were considered and 26% of male Lecturers were considered.

19 candidates were considered for promotion from Senior Lecturer to Reader: all were male. Nine candidates were successful. 11% of male Senior Lecturers were considered.

It will be noted that there are 177 male Senior Lecturers and 10 female Senior Lecturers.

Wastage

No reliable information is available at this stage to enable a proper analysis of the rate and reason for wastage. The Equal Opportunities Unit has designed a two-tier system (ie. questionnaire and, if appropriate, exit interview) to collect information to allow effective monitoring of wastage. This system will, hopefully, be fully operational from the beginning of 1991.

Conclusion

Males are disproportionally represented amongst academic staff, a situation which is common throughout the United Kingdom. Further, female staff are concentrated in the lower grades. There is a trend of increasing representation amongst females and a large percentage of female staff are under 40 years of age, although the rate of promotion amongst females is lower than that for males. However, as expected, there would appear not to be any failure to provide equality of opportunity at the point of selection.

What the analysis has shown is that there is a significant imbalance re gender. To some extent the current problem is a result of historical factors and in the past women have been conspicuous by their absence from the academic staff. This considerable under-representation is slowly changing and ever more women now seem to view the academic life as a serious option as a career path. But it must be stressed that this change is very slow and measures will be sought to expedite it. Progress will be hampered unless ways are found to increase the rate of applications from women. It is also important that women are fairly represented in the more senior grades. While increased representation at lower levels should bring about this result, it is worrying that women seem to have a proportionally lower rate of promotion than men.

We have a situation which is improving naturally, but we can assist and speed up change by positive action. Aside from the moral aspect, it is in the best interests of universities that potential (female) staff are encouraged to consider employment there. With a greater pool of applicants, the University is given a wider choice and this limits the prospect of losing a useful addition to the academic staff to either another University or to another career.

The QUB Equal Opportunities Unit hopes to produce a full report on the position of female academics within the near future, which will recommend specific positive action measures designed to remedy identifiable problems relating to the provision of equality of opportunity, Such positive action measures will be designed following consultation with all relevant personnel within the University and with the Equal Opportunities Commission.

It is the intention of the Unit to identify other areas of under-representation and carry out similar analyses with a view to affirmative action. We hope that we can commence shortly on a detailed analysis of administrative and clerical grades re religious and gender breakdown.

In summary may I give some insights into this area which I feel may be of use:-

1. It is not enough to have lofty Policy Statements if the intention is not galvanised into positive action which is results-orientated.

2. Let staff know what you are doing and why - there will be a lot of suspicion regarding your intentions and confusion over what goals and timetables mean.

3. Train key staff in equal opportunity issues.

4. Sell yourself and your concepts - don't forget that good public relations can overcome a lot of antagonism and suspicion; there will be both.

5. Go for an early success and make it known - this will give the work of your committees/unit credibility.

6. You may see yourselves as the moral conscience of the organisation   but this seldom proves a successful argument in bringing about change.   Use whatever arguments work e.g.   it makes financial sense to exploit the labour market to the full and to recruit and retain the best people.

7. Tailor your positive action programmes to particular problems which have been highlighted by monitoring. Review their success and adapt accordingly.

8. Try not to be seen as always the bearer of bad tidings.

WOMEN AND WOMEN'S STUDIES IN HIGHER EDUCATION IN IRELAND: PROMOTING EQUAL OPPORTUNITIES THROUGH NETWORKING

Dearbhal Ni Charthaigh

[This paper explores the possible structure within which the twin goals of equal opportunities in employment in academe and the development of women's studies, can be pursued.

Ed.]

I am very grateful to Professor Maire Mulcahy and to the organisers of this forum at University College Cork for the opportunity to speak on a topic which has concerned me for some years now.   A concern with access to higher education and with the content of that education is not new, but in the 1980's we emphasised different features of our participation in higher education. Those features include a concern for all women workers in third level institutions, with Women's Studies, and with access not merely to higher education as students but also to employment in academic posts at all levels.

Our concerns show how the situation had improved since the 1880's when formal access to higher education was denied to women, and where the pool of women educated to a matriculation level was extremely small in any case. Even then, universal education was a considerable improvement on the situation described by Hannah Woolley in the 19th Century when in a spirited argument for higher education for women she says:

"The Right Education of the Female Sex, as it is in a manner everywhere neglected, so it ought to be generally lamented. Most in this depraved Age think a woman learned and wise enough if she can distinguish her husband's bed from anothers" (Kinnaird, 1979).

The 1880's were years of great activism by supporters of Higher Education for women. By 1886, this university, then called the Queen's College Cork, admitted its first five women students. In the President's report for that year, it was remarked that "their presence contributed greatly to the preservation of order" and it was hoped that "their example will stimulate the men to more attentive and regular work" (Breathnach, 1987).

The 1980's were years of renewed activism on the part of women in higher education and produced an impressive array of organisations and activities. We were no longer concerned with the removal of formal barriers to access but rather with changing the nature of the production and transmission of knowledge in the universities and colleges. Convinced of the truth of the statement that the way a society organises and transmits its knowledge "reflects both the distribution of power and the principles of social control" (Bernstein, 1975) we set about developing woman-centred knowledge both within and outside the formal educational structures.

Among the developments in the 80's were the establishment of the Women's Studies Association of Ireland in 1984, and later, of the special interest groups of the WSAI, two of which had a particular relevance for Higher Education; the Feminist History Forum, and the Women in Higher Education Network (WHEN), to which I will refer in greater detail later. The Women's Studies Forum in U.C.D. and the Women's Studies Unit at the Irish Foundation for Human Development, were also products of the 1980's. The number of publications increased rapidly over the decade and included newsletters, reviews in Women's Studies and scholarly publications. In 1987, the Women's World's Congress was held in Dublin giving a very high profile to women in Higher Education and to Women's Studies but also highlighting the divide, both real and imagined, between women academics and women in other fields of activism. By the end of the decade, we had achieved what had seemed impossible, and the first graduate programme in Women's Studies had started in the University of Limerick, to be joined this year by programmes in U.C.D. and Trinity.

Parallel to these curricular concerns was the question of women's employment in academic institutions, brought into the spotlight by Ailbhe Smyth's study (Smyth, 1984), and developed further by the HEA (1987). In 1987, I initiated the Women in Higher Education Network, and invited interested members of the Women's Studies Association of Ireland to meet in Dublin. After an inaugural meeting at which Celia Davies, Professor of Women's Opportunities in the University of Ulster, addressed the issues of equal opportunities in higher education, we agreed to establish a network and circulate information on:

(a)   the status of equal opportunities policies and practices in each of the Higher Education Institutions North and South;

(b)   developments in curricula including Women's Studies courses.

To date, I have collected and circulated information on a number of universities. This initiative has been completely unfunded, and all the work of maintaining a database of 90 names in the interested institutions and circularising them has been voluntary. I therefore was delighted when Professor Maire Mulcahy broached with me the question of a new initiative, a Forum on equal opportunities issues in the Higher Education colleges.

I believe that the 90's must have a new emphasis in our work in equal opportunities. While the work on curriculum must continue, it is apparent to me that making inroads there, has proved much easier, than improving the balance of women and men in posts of authority in Higher Education. In this we are not alone and I will refer to a major recent research study undertaken in the United States by Chamberlain.

"While there has been much progress for women in Higher Education on the whole, there are two critical areas in which progress over the last 15 years has been slow or halting. One is the representation of women in faculty and administrative positions at the policy-making level. The other is the rate of enrollment of minority women and their rate of advance as faculty members and administrators" (p. 366)

The percentage of women full-time academics in the United States increased from 22% in the early 1970's to 27% in the early 1980's but most of this increase was accounted for by untenured positions in the less prestigious colleges. There was an increase from 9.8% to 10.7% in full professorships in the same period - an imperceptible rise. The increase in administrative positions held by women was more satisfactory (from 23% to 30%), but the salary differentials between men and women in both administrative and academic jobs widened in this period. The representation of minority women in academe is not well documented, but remains extremely low. Unfortunately the American study does not present us with data on women workers in academic institutions other than the categories just mentioned.

As Ph.D. qualifications are one of the best indicators of the pool of qualified applicants for academic posts, and women obtained 35% of these in 1986 in the U.S.A., it is reasonable to expect that the minimum target figure there for women in academic posts should be 36% in the 1990's. In Ireland the figure in 1985 was 29.2%. Should we too consider a target for the 90's and seek the means to ensure that it is attained? This would mean a doubling of the posts held by women in many of our institutions.

If we were to pursue these questions on a collective basis, it is important to note that we would do so in the context of support from a number of agencies. In other words, we would be acting in accordance with principles enunciated by the Government and by the H.E.A. Committee on the Position of Women Academics. Furthermore, we would be in sympathy with the Resolution of the Council of Ministers of the European Community of June 5, 1985 in which an Action Programme on equal opportunities in education was agreed. Item 7 of this programme refers to "Developing a balance between men and women holding positions of responsibility in education". The improvement in balance should cover both the subjects taught and the levels of posts occupied. Education however in this context, does not include Higher Education, which is classified as training in European Community policy.

Returning to the question of the content of Higher Education, I would like to draw your attention to an important initiative by Mrs O'Rourke, Minister for Education, during the Irish Presidency of the European Council of Ministers. At her request, I presented a paper to the Education Committee of the European Community in January 1990, on the question of equal opportunities in teacher education. In that paper I stressed the necessity of bridging the gap between theory and practice, between equal opportunities actions and Women's Studies research. In the set of conclusions prepared by the Irish Presidency on the basis of my paper and agreed by the Council of Ministers on May 31st the following was agreed:

> "[That] the development of Women's Studies and research on gender issues in appropriate research institutions in particular in higher education institutions in the Member States should be encouraged and the links between those involved in such studies and research and those responsible for the training of teachers should be strengthened".

This, the first reference to women's studies in E.C. policy documents to my knowledge, is being followed up by the Equal Opportunities Unit of the Commission of the European Communities now in the planning for the third action programme on equal opportunities for women.

While the text of the third action programme is still under discussion, we can expect to see Women's Studies included specifically with reference to research centres, exchanges of information and experience, and the development of chairs and departments.

This is all highly satisfactory, but we must ensure that these advances are capitalised upon by collective action, and I therefore come now to my final section in which the nature of possible collaboration in a network is discussed.

Mary Daly defines a network as a "tapestry of connections woven and rewoven by Spinsters and Websters; the Net which breaks the fall of Journeyers experiencing the Earthquake Phenomenon and Springing us into New Space" (Daly and Caputi, 1988).

Now while I enjoy that definition enormously (and understand it only partially) I doubt if it would be a very acceptable definition to those whom I would wish to see funding our network enterprise, and I most emphatically wish to see that network funded.

I do not wish to labour over what follows, but to identify very quickly and briefly some of the features of a possible organisation to pursue the twin goals of equal opportunities in employment in academe and Women's Studies in the curriculum of Higher Education.

1. We need a formal not an informal network.

2. The network should be representative of Higher Education in all of Ireland.

3. The network should be funded by the Higher Education institutions as part of their equality programmes.

4. Participation in the network by staff should be seen as a legitimate and important matter, to be undertaken like other committee work and not in free-time such as night-time, weekends.

5. Additional support should be sought from the Commission of the European Communities for networking with comparable organisations in the European Community and for specific actions such as meetings and conferences.

6. The network should have the services of a secretariat within one of the institutions, initially perhaps in U.C.C.

7. There should be a rotation of venues, with each institution hosting in turn meetings, seminars and conferences.

8. Activities should include:

-   co-ordinating further research on such issues as,
    the life cycle and careers of married, single and
    childless academics; who has a disproportionate
    share of teaching loads? What rewards are
    available for teaching? Is it part of a promotions
    structure? Is research on women given due
    recognition or penalised? Who has access to
    information about institutional research
    resources and opportunities? Should quotas or
    affirmative action policies be introduced and
    how?

-   keeping a record of the progress of equal
    opportunities programmes within the
    institutions, including such questions as the
    provision of statistical data;

-   providing a Newsletter with contact addresses,
    items on equal opportunities policies and
    curriculum in the institutions of Higher
    Education information on conferences and
    publications;

-   preparing and updating a Register of research on
    gender.

9. Liaison with Trade Unions on matters of common
    concern.

These and other suggestions will be pursued in the sessions
tomorrow, and I am looking forward to hearing your views
and suggestions, and particularly to hearing what role you
are prepared to play in such a new organisation.

REFERENCES

1. Bernstein, B. (1975) In: Young, M., Knowledge and Control, Macmillan, London.

2. Breatnach, E. (1987) "Girls Don't Do Honours", Cullen, M. (Ed.) WEB, Dublin.

3. Daly, M. in cahoots with J. Caputi. (1988). Webster's First New Intergalactic Wickedary of the English Language, Attic Press.

4. Kinnaird, J.K. (1979) "Mary Astell and the Conservative Contribution to English Feminism". Journal of British Studies, 19, 53.

5. Smyth, A. (1984) Breaking the Circle E.C. Action Programme on Equal Opportunities for Women. National Advisory Group.

6. Smyth, A.N.D. (1987) Women Academics in Ireland. Department of Education and Higher Education Authroity.

7. Women Academics in Ireland: (1987) Report of the Committee on the Position of Women Academics in Third Level Education in Ireland, published by Higher Education Authority.

EQUALITY OF OPPORTUNITY OF THIRD LEVEL: THE IMPACT OF SECOND LEVEL CHOICES

Sylvia Meehan

[This presentation illustrates the crucial influence of subject choice at second level on equality in third level education and also in the paid labour market, and argues for a concerted education action programme to address the issues.

Ed.]

The centrality of equality of opportunity and take-up of subject options in formal education, to equality in all aspects of Irish life, is inescapable.

I propose to concentrate first on these questions and then to move on, if I may, to the issue of equality among the providers of education at third level.

The Department of Education and the Higher Education Authority have recently released statistical reports which give an account of patterns in second and third level education in the academic year 1987/1988.

In particular we can see that the traditional imbalances in subject take-up still obtain at second and third level.

SECOND LEVEL

Data related to the take-up of subject options at second level in the Department of Education's report indicate that:
-    of 22,738 students taking higher course mathematics in senior cycle 13,800 (60%) were boys;
-    of 2,189 students taking applied mathematics as an option in senior cycle 1,962 (90%) were boys;
-    of 22,108 students taking physics in senior cycle 16,658 (75%) were boys;
-    of 56,087 students taking biology in senior cycle, 36,310 (65%) were girls;
-    of 7,665 students taking engineering as an option in senior cycle 7,551 (99%) were boys;
-    of 14,793 students taking technical drawing as an option in senior cycle 14,406 (97%) were boys;
-    of 29,615 students taking home economics as an option, 26,961 (91%) were girls.

This level of imbalance related to sex of student in Irish second level schools is unacceptable. The direct result of this pattern is that young Irish men and women emerge from the education system with a different range of skills which characteristics are due to a sex stereotyped system of education.

In that context, therefore, it is hardly surprising that Irish men and women have different experiences in the paid labour market.

THIRD LEVEL

An analysis of the statistics relating to participation in third level education brings home forcefully the role that sex currently plays in determining the paid labour market experience of men and women. In 1987/1988, of 1,070 new entrants to engineering courses at HEA institutions 910 (85%) were men. At the same time 86% of entrants to social science, 78% of entrants to communications and information studies and 63% of entrants to arts faculties, were women.

These statistics emphasise the failure of the Irish education system to remove sex stereotyping influences from the important choices being made by young Irish men and women.

If 90% or more of entrants to a particular course are of the same sex, then it is a reasonable conclusion that the providers of the course have not tackled the problem of stereotyping by sex in that discipline. At third level it is not acceptable for the relevant institutions to rely on the excuse that course entrants make their own choices. Some interventions and recommendations are required.

A new impetus is required to provide an equality of educational provision to young Irish men and women. In that regard, I believe that state and European Community expenditure on education is seriously flawed if the outcome of that expenditure is to reinforce rather than to remove sex-based imbalances in Irish life.

I believe that the education system needs an action programme to ensure that:

Second Level

-    as complete and representative a range of subjects as possible be provided for all school pupils;

-    subjects be available in such a way that they are actually and equally accessible to girls and boys;

87

-   an advisory and information programme is undertaken to advise pupils <u>and their parents</u> of the opportunities and consequences which are dependent on subject choices in second-level education.

Second and Third Level

-   guidance and training for teachers is provided so that they can help boys and girls understand the relationship that exists between personal and educational experiences in school and the pupils' adult role expectations and opportunities. In the past, girls have been expected to under-achieve in Maths and Physical Sciences, and the idea grew up that boys, but not girls, needed skills in these disciplines. That is not realistic for today's world of work or home. Third level institutions have a vital communications role in assistance and linkage to second level;

-   course material is relevant to the interests of both sexes and the presentation, teaching methods and assessment of skills and knowledge are free from sex-bias. Pilot studies show that pupils' interest in a subject increases if the course material relates to something that is already familiar, and is presented in a way that encourages them to feel competent and able to succeed;

-   change is brought about in the shared attitudes and expectations of pupils, parents and teachers and especially in the attitudes of girls. If the general attitude is "girls don't do Physics" it is not surprising that most girls do not opt for Physics, and the old fashioned fear than higher level Maths is somehow "unfeminine" does great disservice to Maths as well as women! Parents and teachers are very familiar with "peer group influence" but a surprising number of them do little to counteract myths about women's abilities, which are then picked up and continued by the younger generation who really need to develop positive attitudes to subject choices, particularly in Science, Mathematics and Technical subjects and with regard to their self perception. Girls frequently demonstrate unrealistic, low self-assessment of their capacity to succeed in non-traditional subject areas, but they would be able to succeed if they were given encouragement and positive feedback.

- Students require to develop positive attitudes with regard to their expectations in the labour market and their employment aspirations which may strongly influence their choice of subjects. Girls need to know that traditional-type women's jobs have decreased and they may not offer good career prospects in the years to come. Many households need two incomes to sustain a family's standard of living and women's job prospects are not confined to a few years between school and marriage.

Such a programme should operate at all levels and sectors of the education system. It would involve, for example:

- a combined national and schools based policy;

- a major information campaign for management, teachers, guidance counsellors and parents;

- a personal development programme for girls and boys which will help them to share parental roles, domestic tasks and vocational responsibilities;

- support for school-level interventions of which there are some excellent examples already in operation;

-    the provision of a centre of advice for school management; and

-    the funding of pilot studies.

These suggestions should be considered by seminar participants as they are basic to "Equality of opportunity in education policy" in general terms. Matters more specific to third level and equality issues among academic staff will be discussed during the panel session.

THE ROAD TO EQUAL OPPORTUNITIES FOR THE WOMEN AND MEN ON THE STAFF IN UNIVERSITY COLLEGE DUBLIN

Helen Burke

[This paper details the process of working towards equal opportunities for female and male staff in University College Dublin from the early 1980's to date.

Ed.]

The process of working for equal opportunities and equal treatment for women and men on the staff in UCD started in the early 1980's in an informal way at the bottom of the UCD hierarchy. It started through channelling knowledge and complaints into action by:

1. **The Women's Studies Forum** an informal alliance of women staff and students from across the University sectors and from outside, coming together regularly to listen to and discuss research papers, poetry or prose on different aspects of women's lives, including our own position in UCD. The Women's Studies Forum provided not only continuing education but also the friendship, support and insights to try to tackle the issue of inequality on wider fronts within our institution. Notices of meetings were posted up around the college and outside. Anyone could come along. The Women's Studies Forum was run by a collective of women in UCD, women from the library, research students and academics. Its broad base was one of its strengths. It got a small grant from college, to help defray the expenses of visiting speakers. From

91

The Women's Studies Forum came the impetus to start formal academic courses in Women's Studies in UCD. The post-graduate programme in Women's Studies began in October 1990.

2.   **Documenting the case:** A series of studies started with Ailbhe Smyth's <u>Breaking the Circle</u>, (1984) which 'painted the picture' of where women were located - at the bottom of the pyramid - across the third level sector in Ireland and in our own institution. This was followed by the Report of the HEA Committee which Prof. Maire Mulcahy of UCC chaired - <u>Women Academics in Ireland</u> (1987) and by Emer Smyth and my report on the position of women in UCD - <u>Distant Peaks: - a Study of The Relative Staffing Levels of Women and Men in University College. Dublin</u>, (1988, an unpublished report for the EC Women's Bureau and the UCD Governing Body). Professor Eunice McCarthy's Study for the EEA, <u>Transitions to Equal Opportunity at Work: Problems and Possibilities</u>, (1986) had convinced us that 'painting the picture' of where men or women were located in the institutional hierarchy was the essential first step to take in trying to change a large traditional institution. Women staff across the University sectors knew their situation well enough. But the lowly position of women in the college's hierarchy was not at first acknowledged as a problem by our male colleagues (with a few honourable exceptions!). So we had to paint and publish the picture if this problem was going to be recognized and put on UCD's agenda for action. (Burke and Smyth, <u>Equality of Opportunity in UCD</u>? 1989).

The Women's Studies Forum provided the solidarity and support for women staff to challenge chauvinistic attitudes at faculty and other fora, e.g. when an eminent

Professor announced at Faculty: "The man we want for this Chair is such and such..." - it was suggested, it was a **person** that was being sought and so forth! We fought to get women on selection boards and onto other bodies where they could influence decisions. With only 16% of the full-time academic staff female, this involves a lot of hard work.

The 1987 - 1990 Governing Body of UCD has 5 women, out of a total of 37 members. Not many, but never before had it so many women! Three of the six members elected by the graduates were women and the two Government nominees were women. Since 1985 the Governing Body has had an Equal Opportunities Committee. It was that Committee that commissioned the study Distant Peaks funded by the EC. That study contained twelve recommendations on an equal opportunities policy for UCD which were accepted by the Governing Body in 1989, when UCD formally committed itself to being an equal opportunities employer (see Appendix A). In 1990, the Governing Body agreed to appoint an Equality Officer/Training and Development Officer to the College. The appointment has not yet been made but it is coming....

Thus, one can conclude by saying that this traditional institution has come to recognise the importance of equal opportunities and equal treatment for the women and men within it; UCD has started down the road towards equal opportunities for its women and men, both students and staff but - there is still much to be done to make it a reality.

APPENDIX A

Recommendations of the Equal Opportunities Sub-committee adopted by the Governing Body of University College Dublin, February, 1989.

1. The EC outlines four stages in a Positive Action Programme (Positive Action: Equal Opportunities for Women in Employment: A Guide, - Luxembourg: Office for Official Publications of the European Communities, 1988). Stage I is the Commitment Stage. This involves the organisation in formally adopting a policy of equal opportunity and publicizing its commitment to its staff and in its public advertisements.

Recommendation I: that the UCD Governing Body commits itself formally to an equal opportunities policy and practice and notifies staff accordingly.

2. One of the problems encountered in the course of this study, (Smyth, E., and Burke, H. *Distant Peaks: A Study of the Relative Staffing Levels of Women and Men in University College Dublin*). was the absence of a Personnel Department in University College Dublin.

    The EC Guide states that: "*A senior officer should assume responsibility for the programme and the resources allocated to it. Important factors to consider when making such an appointment would be the ability, interest and position of the officer involved*".

Recommendation II: that UCD establish a Personnel Department and that one of its most senior staff be appointed Equality Officer with responsibility to implement the positive action programme.

3. The EC Guide recommends the establishment of a co-ordinating group to work with the Equality Officer.

Recommendation III: that the Governing Body formally establish an Equal Opportunities Committee which would work with the Equality Officer in advising the Governing Body on the implementation of policy in this area.

4   The next stage is the Information and Analysis Stage. University College Dublin has already gathered much information in this report (Smyth, *E.* and Burke, H.,' Distant Peaks' *op. cit.)* which also contains an initial analysis of the data. Such information and analysis should, according to the *EC, "lead the organisation to have a close look at its current personnel policies".* Review of Personnel Policies and Practices are crucial, according to the *EC:"When examining personnel policies and practices particular attention should be given to the following areas: (i) recruitment; (ii) promotion; (iii) training; (iv) working conditions . It is important while carrying out this review to bear in mind that it has repeatedly been found that employment policies and practices - which may appear to be neutral and which may be implemented impartially - in fact operate to exclude women for reasons which are not job-related or required for safe or efficient business operation. Care should be taken, therefore, that the seemingly 'invisible' barriers to equal opportunities that may exist within the organization are recognized as such."* (EC Guide *op cit, p. 19)*

Recommendation IV: that the Personnel Department would devise strategies (including additional training) for the removal of practices which operate to exclude women for reasons that are not job-related.

5.   It is envisaged that the presentation of this report to the Governing Body will move UCD into the **Action Stage**. A crucial part of this stage, according to the EC, is in job assignment and promotion. According to the EC Guide: "A necessary step to take in order to get a more even distribution of men and women at all levels of the workforce, is to broaden access or open career paths to women.

Job assignment and, in particular, first job placement is of crucial importance and can be a decisive factor in whether or not an employee has promotion opportunities throughout his/her career. Even when their qualifications are equivalent to those of their male colleagues, it appears that women - more than men - get a first job placement in so-called 'dead end jobs' where their progress possibilities are slim. (The U.C.D. report, Smyth, E. and Burke, H. op. cit., confirms this and the subcommittee sees the need for action to develop career paths).

"It is extremely important, therefore, to find ways of giving all employees the chance to progress according to their ability in the organisation. Further useful measures in the context of promotion are to: (i) Give all employees access to vacancies and ensure, where appropriate, that all vacancy information is circulated within the organisation. (ii) Include women in informal advice of vacancies occurring. (iii) On a general level encourage internal transfer of an employee - male or female - to a job where that sex is under- represented."

Recommendation V: that a job description be prepared for all vacancies occurring within the College and be circulated within the college as well as advertised outside (when this is appropriate);

6. **Recommendation VI: that women staff be encouraged to apply for promotional posts, particularly to those areas where women are poorly represented;**

7. **Recommendation VII: that the candidates be made aware of the procedures, including the dates of meetings, of the relevant committees and the criteria for promotion;**

8. **Recommendation VIII: that, where possible, training opportunities be developed to facilitate staff to move out of dead end jobs.**

9. The EC also provides the following advice on interviewing for either recruitment or promotion: *"A very useful step to take here would be to brief interviewers so as to achieve a standard policy devoid of discriminatory practices. It would also be helpful to make available a manual on interview conduct based on the principles of equal opportunities, including amongst others the following criteria:*

    (i) Do not make assumptions about women workers ! (ii) Interview men and women in the same way with objective selection criteria. (iii) Avoid asking questions about marital status, childcare arrangements, or any other questions unrelated to job requirements. (iv) Avoid using patronising phrases, no matter how kindly the words are meant (i.e. 'dear 'love etc.; (v)

Include women on interview panels (E.C. Guide op. cit. p.22). We know from our survey that women applying for jobs in UCD are still, on occasions, asked personal questions about their domestic arrangements.

Recommendation IX: that a guide to non-discriminatory interview practice be drawn up and made available to all members of interview boards and that normally both sexes be included on such boards.

10. A combination of factors emerged from this research that suggest that UCD needs to be more responsive to married women staff and women staff with children. These are: only 16% of full-time academic staff are women; of these academic women only 39% are married and 61% of women academics do not have children; the career pattern of women academics is broadly similar to that of men; no married women or women with children are in the senior grades of administration. These findings suggest that, for whatever reason, UCD is either not recruiting, retaining or promoting married female staff and is, in many cases, losing the contribution such people could make to the life of the college. UCD has a good creche, but it also needs to develop other new policies and practices so that the potential contribution of this group is not lost to the college.

Recommendation X: that UCD examine its policies towards married women and women with children to ensure that they are not discriminated against at recruitment and promotion interviews and that greater flexibility be developed in working arrangements, such as career breaks and job-sharing, so that women with children are not deterred from pursuing their careers.

11.   The EC Guide stresses the importance of: *"Effective monitoring and regular assessment of the positive action programme, just as they are essential for any other company programme. They enable the organization to: (i) assess progress towards goals; (ii) see where success is being achieved; (iii) identify the need to correct or adjust undesirable developments.*

It is important, therefore, that information on the progress of action undertaken is recorded so that adequate assessment of the effect and development of positive action in the organisation can be made." (EC Guide, op cit, p.29)

Recommendation XI: that this UCD positive action - equal opportunities programme be regularly monitored, e.g. that information on the applicants and appointments for both recruitment and promotional posts be collected and analysed by gender and be made available to the Governing Body on an annual basis, and that the Governing Body receive an annual report on the overall progress of the programme.

12.   However, before that can be done, UCD needs to get its information base in order.

Recommendation XII: that in future the President's Annual Report presents information on Administrative, Library, Technical and other staff by grade and gender, as it currently does for the academic staff.

ACHIEVING REAL EQUALITY OF OPPORTUNITY IN AN ACADEMIC ENVIRONMENT: RECENT EXPERIENCE AT TRINITY COLLEGE DUBLIN

Frances Ruane

[This paper reviews the position of women students and staff in Trinity College Dublin since the first woman student was admitted in 1904, and outlines the recent initiatives which have been taken in that College to promote equality of opportunity.

Ed.]

INTRODUCTION

Writing in their history of Trinity College, published in 1982, R.B. McDowell and D.A. Webb commented that:

> even the most ardent feminist can scarcely claim in 1980, that at least as far as formal regulations are concerned, women are at any disadvantage in College compared with men.

Certainly in 1980 even the most strident feminist could not disagree with Professors McDowell and Webb, because, as far as *formal regulations* were concerned, the situation was certainly one of equality of opportunity for men and women in Trinity College. The issue under discussion in the College in recent years has centred on whether or not male and female academics operate, *de facto* as well as *de jure*, on equal terms.

The process whereby women have become full members of Trinity College has taken almost 100 years, starting with the College's providing examinations for female students enrolled at Alexandra College in 1870, and continuing with the admission of the first woman student in 1904 and the appointment of the first woman academic for 1909. It took a further 60 years for all areas of academic life to be opened up on equal terms to both males and females and, as McDowell and Webb note, it was not without considerable reluctance, at almost every stage, on the part of some male academics in the College. According to McDowell and Webb there are many examples of attitudes changing very slowly and reluctantly on the issue of increased equality for women in Trinity College. For example as recently as 1964, in the debate on admitting women to Fellowship, A.A. Luce, one of the Senior Fellows is said to have argued that "for a married woman domestic duties were apt to increase gradually but insidiously, until these were sufficient to prevent her from conscientiously carrying out the duties of a full-time post" (op. cit. p. 363). The authors also point to the key role played by the individual Provosts and Senior Fellows in promoting or undermining the cause of women in Trinity College. They suggest that the role of Provosts especially has been crucial.

As Trinity College approaches its quartercentenary the process whereby female students have integrated into College is now complete, with there being no significant difference in the proportion of male and female under-graduates in the College, though there are obviously still differences among individual subject areas. The situation with regard to academics is still very unequal in terms of representation, with full-time male academics greatly outnumbering female academics, especially at senior levels. This high degree of unequal representation is not uncommon in universities, and in the case of Trinity College the low level of overall female representation can in part be explained by the rapid expansion in staff numbers in the 1970s when, compared with the present, relatively fewer women were qualified for posts in many academic areas. Nonetheless, in 1988 concern over the low level of female representation on the staff, almost 80 years after the appointment of the first female academic, led to the formation of an *ad hoc* committee of women academics, which submitted a proposal to the Board of Trinity College on behalf of 49 women academics that it should establish a special committee of the Board to examine "the position of women academics in College."

ESTABLISHMENT OF A COMMITTEE ON THE POSITION OF WOMEN ACADEMICS

The Board approved the establishment of such a committee in November 1988 and approved the nominated committee, consisting of ten academics representing all faculties in College, in January 1989.

The Committee met on six occasions and considered a wide variety of material including:

Data on the career patterns of 42 female and 36 male academics in College, taken from a survey by the HEA of all female academics and a matched sample of male academics in all third-level colleges in Ireland in 1985/6;

Submissions from 25 members of the academic staff in College: all full-time, and from a number of part time: as many part-time staff as it was possible to contact were invited to make submissions;

Documents from the Staff Office on recruitment and promotion in College;

Information on the operation of the Day Nursery and Nursery School;

Report of the First Stage of the Pilot Programme on the Promotion of Positive Action for Women in University College Dublin, September 1988;

HEA Report on the Position of Women Academics in Third Level Education in Ireland, 1987;

Affirmative Action: Guidelines for Implementation in Institutions of Higher Education, 1987, Australian Government Publication.

In addition, individual members of the Committee also met with various interested parties, including members of the Staff Office, the Supervisor of the Day Nursery, the Bursar, the Senior Dean, the Registrar and members of the Committee on Student Discipline.

The data from the Staff Office for 1988/89 which was analysed by the Committee showed that full-time male academics outnumbered female academics generally by four to one and at senior levels by twenty to one, and that there has been little sign of improvement over the 1980s. Indeed, the position would have deteriorated further over the 1980s had the College not extended its range of disciplines to cover Occupational Therapy where the staff are all female. (Table I) The Committee noted, with reference to the HEA report that, in terms of seniority, the representation of women at higher levels in College was slightly better than the Irish university average in 1984/5, where the percentages of women at the different grades were professor (2 per cent), associate professor (5 per cent) and senior lecturer (7 per cent) respectively. Nonetheless, the Committee argued that such a degree of under-representation in College generally, and at the upper grades in particular, merited the attention of a serious investigation into why women are so under-represented. It was agreed that under-representation did not necessarily represent deliberate discrimination, and concluded that *there appears to be no evidence of a pattern of deliberate discrimination against women academics in Trinity College.* However, the Committee identified areas in which women academics may be implicitly receiving less favourable treatment than their male colleagues, and proposed a series of policy recommendations which, while not discriminating against men, would help remove obstacles to, and support the recruitment and promotion of, more women academics.

THE POLICY RECOMMENDATIONS ACCEPTED

In June 1989 the Committee presented its report to the Board. Some 34 recommendations were made in it and most of these have been accepted and acted upon by the College administration during the past 12 months. The recommendations accepted can be grouped under a number of headings.

General Ethos

The Committee recommended that the College indicate formally its commitment to equality of opportunity by formally amending the statutes and by establishing a permanent Committee to monitor equality of opportunity in the College. Both of these recommendations are presently being implemented, though the College administration has only conceded that the permanent committee would address equality issues among permanent full-time academics.

College Government

The Committee recommended greater democratisation of College committees and increased employment of women academics as tutors (mentors) where this is possible. These recommendations are being implemented, though in an *ad hoc* way; in particular, committee nominees are still selected rather haphazardly, and the College administration has shied away from the suggestion of drawing-up a list of academics who have indicated their willingness to serve on particular committees.

Recruitment and Promotion

The Committee recommended that there should be representation of both sexes on each appointment committee, and that all members of each committee are entitled to full access to all documentation and all procedures relevant to the appointment. Both of these recommendations were accepted and the College's Academic Council set out in detail the procedures for appointing all academic staff. In response to other recommendations the College has also revised its application forms to exclude questions relating to marital and parental status, and has introduced a statement in advertisements for all academic posts to the effect that it is an equal opportunities employer.

Employment Contracts

In its deliberations the Committee noted that the working conditions of many part-time employees in the College were not very satisfactory, and that many of the part-timers, for whom employment in the College was their main or sole source of income, were women. The dissatisfaction expressed by such staff related far more to the lack of adequate library, parking and accommodation rights than to rates of pay. The College administration accepted the Committee's recommendation that a separate committee should be established to examine the position of part-time academics, and this committee is due to convene at the start of the 1990 academic term.

Maternity Leave and Childcare

The Committee recommended the establishment of standard procedures for maternity leave, so that women seeking such leave were in no way dependent for replacement simply on the good nature of their head of department or their departmental colleagues. The College accepted this recommendation in general terms though it would not agree to automatically granting full replacement resources, as it was argued that the need for such resources varied across different departments.

The College agreed to implement a set of recommendations for the improvement of day-care facilities for the children of staff and students and improved management of the resources provided for this purpose by the College.

THE POLICY RECOMMENDATIONS PENDING/NOT ACCEPTED

While the Committee was very pleased that many of its recommendations were accepted, there were some which have either received outright rejection or are still pending with major modifications. Again these are best viewed under general headings.

General Ethos

The Committee asked for an explicit commitment by the College administration to reducing sexism in College: (i) by removing all sexist language from documentation relating tò staff and students; and (ii) by publicly criticising any sexist attitudes which might be voiced by academics in College. The administration has agreed to implement (i) as documents come up for revision, but there seems to be a certain reluctance on (ii). It seemed to the Committee that a statement should be issued by the Provost and Board to the effect that sexist attitudes are completely unacceptable in TCD in the 1990s, in order to raise the awareness of those who are implicitly or explicitly sexist in their attitudes to staff and/or students.

Recruitment and Promotion

The Committee sought a balance of male and female members on all promotions committees. Unfortunately the complex system of promotion committees in TCD makes it impossible for the College administration to enforce the inclusion of a woman on the promotions committees as currently constituted, since all of the appointments are either *ex officio* or elected appointments. The Committee asked that this issue be raised with the nominating groups and this is now in train through the Committee on Equal Opportunities for Academics.

The Committee asked that a research seminar should automatically be a part of the recruiting procedure and this was, to its surprise strongly rejected by many Board members, though supported personally by the Provost. The Committee argued that such seminars were a matter of good recruitment practice and would draw attention to the importance of teaching and presentation, making sure that, as far as possible, all elements in the job specification for an academic post were evaluated as fairly as possible. All nominating committees will continue to have, as at present, the option to arrange for such seminars.

Maternity Leave

The Committee recommended to the Board that women academics whose children are born during the summer vacation, thereby interrupting research time rather than teaching time, should have some reduction in their subsequent teaching loads, in order to make up for the lost research time and to re-establish a research programme. This recommendation gained absolutely no acceptance at Board, despite the fact that it was recognised that such an academic's research record is the major determinant of her possibilities for promotion.

The Board also refused, on the grounds of financial constraint, to accept the Committee's recommendation that a policy on dependency and paternity leave should be established.

Sexual Harrassment

The Committee recommended that the College formulate a procedure to deal with sexual harassment in the College, and in particular to determine what constitutes an appropriate definition of sexual harassment in a university environment. This issue caused great unease at the Board, as though reference to the potential problem (which is acknowledged in universities worldwide) was either in poor taste or irrelevant because the problem was simply unknown in the College. In the past year there has been a hesitant recognition of the need to deal with the issue, and steps are finally underway to determine an appropriate definition of harassment.

Women in Non-Academic Jobs

The Committee recommended that the Board establish other committees to examine the position of women employed in non-academic jobs in College. This won absolutely no support at Board, which accused the Committee of going beyond its brief. However the Board conceded that it would not refuse to consider any requests for the establishment of similar review committees from other groups of women in College.

OUTLOOK FOR THE FUTURE

The outlook for equality of opportunity in Trinity College depends crucially on two factors: (a) the willingness of the College to implement policies which will create an environment in which male and female academics operate *de facto* on equal terms and (b) the opportunity available to

110

the College to employ and promote more female academics.

(a) The progress made in TCD in terms of establishing a
     basis for greater equality of opportunity in the past
     year has been considerable, and there is now greater
     awareness of the issue throughout College. However,
     what is striking and disappointing is that the College,
     as an academic institution, does not seem to be taking
     any leadership in this area. An example of this lack of
     leadership is the resistance to the recommendation to
     review the position of women in non-academic jobs in
     College. Indeed, to ensure that the institution is
     genuinely non-sexist, women in *all* areas of the College
     must be treated as equals with men in their relevant
     peer groups; it is not sufficient that such rights be
     accorded to students and full-time academic staff only.
     Other examples of non-leadership were evident in (i)
     the attitudes expressed to providing women with time-
     off from teaching where maternity leave coincides with
     the vacation, (ii) the failure to guarantee automatic
     resources for replacement of teaching staff on
     maternity leave and (iii) the resistance to admit to the
     possibility that the College might need a set of
     procedures to deal with sexual harassment, over and
     above the disciplinary procedures already in place.
     Finally there was a general resistance to any
     arguments which suggested that the College
     administration should take some responsibility for
     changing attitudes in College. For example,
     recommendations that the College officers should
     encourage heads of departments to make an effort to
     look for potential female applicants for academic posts
     and to ensure that potential female graduates are
     properly counselled were more or less ignored, as if
     these were simply unnecessary. These attitudes
     prevailed despite the fact that it is widely recognised

that one of the greatest disadvantages for potential women academics is that they are not part of the traditional "academic network", and such actions are necessary to overcome this disadvantage.

(b) With the expansion in student numbers and the associated increase in academic staff numbers the opportunity for the College to employ and promote more female academics is better now than it has been in more than a decade. This year the number of full-time academic staff will rise for the first time since 1979. Because of the age/gender structure in the College, it is inevitable that the majority of those who reach retirement each year are male academics, so the improvement in the representation of women depends crucially on the gender pattern at recruitment. The information available to date on recruitments this year is very promising: 40 per cent of the 30 posts filled by 28 August have gone to women. Furthermore of the 12 posts filled by women, seven are in areas where the participation rates of female academics have traditionally been very low (Medicine, Science and Engineering). While the effect of this on the overall proportion of women among the full-time academic staff is still small (increasing the proportion of women to almost 19 per cent) these rates suggest that more suitably qualified women are available for academic posts.

With increasing staff numbers, it should be possible to increase the numbers promoted without increasing the ratio of senior to junior staff. On the data currently available, 44 per cent of all full-time posts are at the lecturer grade, but the percentage of females on that grade is almost twice that of males (72 per cent compared with 34). With increasing numbers of

112

women entering the lecturer grade, the next decade should see a substantial increase in the absolute numbers of women at senior levels.

Women academics in Trinity College have been fortunate in the past number of years in having a Provost who is supportive of their position, but unfortunate in that the possibilities for increased recruitment and promotion have been very limited. However, while having more posts and a supportive Provost are essential for change, they are not sufficient. Progress in Trinity College in the next few years will also depend on a continuing improvement in the attitude of senior academics to supporting the College's commitment to genuine equality of opportunity.

TABLE I

Number of Full-Time Staff in Each Grade (T.C.D.)

Grade	1984/85				1988/89			
	Males		Females		Males		Females	
	No.	%	No.	%	No.	%	No.	%
Professor	59	95.2	3	4.8	52	94.5	3	5.5
Ass. Professor	35	94.6	2	5.4	40	97.6	1	2.4
Sen. Lecturer	98	92.5	8	7.5	117	90.7	12	9.3
Lecturer	156	72.9	58	27.1	124	70.9	51	29.1
TOTAL	345	82.9	71	17.1	333	83.2	67	16.8
Fellows	128	97.0	4	3.0	132	96.4	5	3.6